W9-BBF-167

Langston Hughes:

The Harlem Renaissance

Writers and Their Works

Langston Hughes:
The Harlem Renaissance

MAURICE WALLACE

Marshall Cavendish
Benchmark
New York

for Sage and Amaya,
whose souls live the dreams of the ancestors

I could not have completed this short book on Langston Hughes without the limitless generosity of several people. First, I thank Michelle Bisson of Marshall Cavendish for her extreme patience, encouragement, and a remarkable confidence in me. For assisting me in research and other items preparatory to this book, I owe Jason Hendrickson of the University of Massachusetts at Amherst. I am also profoundly indebted to Alisha Damron, Alisha Gaines, Alexis Gumbs, and Elaine Yee, all of Duke University, for their support during the most pressing periods when this work was under construction. They assisted me, of course, but honored the memory of Langston Hughes more significantly. Finally, I cannot thank my family enough for accommodating my impossible schedule and excusing me from many of our terrific family outings to complete this work. Humbly, I dedicate this work to them.

Marshall Cavendish Benchmark
99 White Plains Road
Tarrytown, NY 10591
www.marshallcavendish.us

Library of Congress Cataloging-in-Publication Data
Wallace, Maurice O. (Maurice Orlando), 1967-
Langston Hughes : the Harlem Renaissance / by Maurice Wallace.
p. cm. — (Writers and their works)
Summary: "A biography of writer Langston Hughes that describes his era, his major works—especially his most famous and influential prose and poetry, his life, and and the legacy of his writing"—Provided by publisher.
Includes bibliographical references (p.) and index.
ISBN 978-0-7614-2591-5
1. Hughes, Langston, 1902-1967—Juvenile literature. 2. Poets, American—20th century—Biography—Juvenile literature. 3. African American poets—Biography—Juvenile literature. I. Title. II. Series.
PS3515.U274Z93 2007
818'.5209—dc22 2006038162

All poems by permission, Random House. See page 144 for credits.

Photo research by Linda Sykes Picture Research, Hilton Head, SC

George Eastman House. Gift of the Muray family 77:0189:1477: Cover, 2, 6; Beinecke Library/ Yale University: 12, 33, 39, 40, 53, 62, 82, 84, 91, 96, 111; National Portrait Gallery, Smithsonian Institution/Art Resource, NY ©2007 Estate of Carl Van Vechten: 45; ©Bettmann/Corbis: 59; Digital Image ©The Museum of Modern Art/ Licensed by SCALA/Art Resource, NY ©2007 Estate of Jacob Lawrence/Artists Rights Society (ARS), NY: 66; The Jacob and Gwendolyn Lawrence Foundation/Art Resource, NY ©2007 Estate of Jacob Lawrence/Artists Rights Society (ARS), NY: 70; Photographs and Prints Division, Schomburg Center for Research in Black Culture, The New York Public Library, Astor, Lenox and Tilden Foundations: 73; ©Schomburg Center for Research in Black Culture, The New York Public Library, New York/Art Resource, NY. ©The Aaron and Alta Douglas Foundation, Kansas: 74; Library of Congress: 106.

Publisher: Michelle Bisson
Art Director: Anahid Hamparian
Series Designer: Sonia Chaghatzbanian

Printed in China
1 3 5 6 4 2

s And can't be satisfied— I ain't happy no mo' And I wi
t the Weary Blues And can't be satisfied— I ain't happy
e satisfied. Got the Weary Blues And can't be satisfied-
ie And I can't be satisfied. Got the Weary Blues And ca:

Contents

isfied— I ain't happy no mo' And I wish that I had died.
d can't be satisfied— I ain't happy no mo' And I wish th
: Weary Blues And can't be satisfied— I ain't happy no
satisfied. Got the Weary Blues And can't be satisfied-
ie And I can't be satisfied. Got the Weary Blues And ca
got the Weary Blue And I can't be satisfied. Got the Wee
I had died.""I got the Weary Blue And I can't be satisfie
I I wish that I had died.""I got the Weary Blue And I ca
happy no mo' And I wish that I had died.""I got the Wee
isfied— I ain't happy no mo' And I wish that I had died.
d can't be satisfied— I ain't happy no mo' And I wish t

can't be satisfied— I ain't happy no mo' And I wish that
"I got the Weary Blue And I can't be satisfied. Got the
s And can't be satisfied— I ain't happy no mo' And I

't happy no mo' And I wish that I had died.""I got the
And I can't be satisfied. Got the Weary Blues And ca
fied— I ain't happy no mo' And I wish that I had died."
eary Blue And I can't be satisfied. Got the Weary Blues
be satisfied— I ain't happy no mo' And I wish that
"I got the Weary Blue And I can't be satisfied. Got the

Introduction

"I, too, sing America.
I am the darker brother."
(Langston Hughes, "I, Too," from *Collected Poems*, 46)

LANGSTON HUGHES IS ONE OF THE MOST honored names in twentieth-century American and African-American poetry. His reputation is nearly synonymous with the Harlem Renaissance cultural movement, which began around 1919 and witnessed the flowering of new literary, musical, and artistic talents by a generation of extraordinary African-American artists.

Hughes came on the scene early. He was just nineteen and beginning college at Columbia University when his first major poem, "The Negro Speaks of Rivers," was published in *Crisis* magazine. Although Hughes enjoys a considerable reputation today as one of the most widely read African-American poets of the twentieth century, he fell in and out of the public's favor during his forty years of writing. His dedication to promoting the blues as a poetic form, for instance, displeased many African Americans who considered the blues an expression of the most low-down and least flattering segment of the race. At least one of Hughes's poems, "Goodbye, Christ," which he intended as a critique of Christian hypocrisy, threatened his career years after it was published. Ultimately, its misinterpretation as an anti-Christian propaganda poem led to Hughes having to testify—to his profound embarrassment—before the infamous Senator Joseph McCarthy and the Senate Permanent Subcommittee on Investigations. He faced charges of anti-American activity and communist sympathizing. It was 1953, the height of the "red scare" in the United States. Hughes was roundly criticized by Americans of all stripes. At certain times, Hughes was so severely maligned that his reputation's recovery from the "gutter-most" (once a black critic called him a "sewer dweller") to the uttermost of black poetic regard represents an extraordinary reversal of fortunes in American literary history.

Today, Hughes's importance to African-American literature and culture is unquestioned. His sensitive ear for black speech and music helped lend poetic voice to the subtle black difference that, according to Henry Louis Gates Jr., distinguishes the African-American literary tradition from traditional white American writing. Hughes's poems have been remembered and recited by four or five generations of American youth and adults in school assemblies, church programs, civic events, graduation exercises, and African American History Month observances. For many, especially African Americans, Hughes has achieved the status of cultural icon, a man lionized and venerated as the black poet laureate of the twentieth century.

At the time of his death in 1967, at age sixty-five, he had not yet retired from writing. After numerous books of verse, a two-volume autobiography, several short stories, two novels, a dozen books for children, twenty years' worth of newspaper columns for the *Chicago Defender*, and scores of plays, musicals, and operettas, Hughes, in a sense, died writing. It was as if, to Hughes, the bounty of art he had produced since 1921 was not all his soul had to bequeath. And yet, to those who have inherited his bounty, it is a marvel that he managed to leave so much.

the Weary Blue And I can't be satisfied. Got the Weary B
be satisfied— I ain't happy no mo' And I wish that I had
he Weary Blue And I can't be satisfied. Got the Weary B
be satisfied— I ain't happy no mo' And I wish that I had
he Weary Blue And I can't be satisfied. Got the Weary B
be satisfied— I ain't happy no mo' And I wish that I had
he Weary Blue And I can't be satisfied. Got the Weary B
be satisfied— I ain't happy no mo' And I wish that I had
he Weary Blue And I can't be satisfied. Got the Weary B
be satisfied— I ain't happy no mo' And I wish that I had
he Weary Blue And I can't be satisfied. Got the Weary B
be satisfied— I ain't happy no mo' And I wish that I had
he Weary Blue And I can't be satisfied. Got the Weary B
be satisfied— I ain't happy no mo' And I wish that I had
he Weary Blue And I can't be satisfied. Got the Weary B
be satisfied— I ain't happy no mo' And I wish that I had
he Weary Blue And I can't be satisfied. Got the Weary B
be satisfied— I ain't happy no mo' And I wish that I had
he Weary Blue And I can't be satisfied. Got the Weary B
be satisfied— I ain't happy no mo' And I wish that I had
he Weary Blue And I can't be satisfied. Got the Weary B
be satisfied— I ain't happy no mo' And I wish that I had
he Weary Blue And I can't be satisfied. Got the Weary B
be satisfied— I ain't happy no mo' And I wish that I had
he Weary Blue And I can't be satisfied. Got the Weary B
be satisfied— I ain't happy no mo' And I wish that I had
he Weary Blue And I can't be satisfied. Got the Weary B
be satisfied— I ain't happy no mo' And I wish that I had
he Weary Blue And I can't be satisfied. Got the Weary B
be satisfied— I ain't happy no mo' And I wish that I ha

at I had died.""I got the Weary Blue And I can't be sat
And I wish that I had died.""I got the Weary Blue And
n't happy no mo' And I wish that I had died.""I got the
satisfied— I ain't happy no mo' And I wish that I had
ues And can't be satisfied— I ain't happy no mo' And I w
t the Weary Blues And can't be satisfied— I ain't happy
satisfied. Got the Weary Blues And can't be satisfied—
ue And I can't be satisfied. Got the Weary Blues And ca
t the Weary Blue And I can't be satisfied. Got the Weary
had died.""I got the Weary Blue And I can't be satisfie
d I wish that I had died.""I got the Weary Blue And I
n't happy no mo' And I wish that I had died.""I got the
satisfied— I ain't happy no mo' And I wish that I had
ues And can't be satisfied— I ain't happy no mo' And I w
t the Weary Blues And can't be satisfied— I ain't happy
satisfied. Got the Weary Blues And can't be satisfied—
ue And I can't be satisfied. Got the Weary Blues And ca
t the Weary Blue And I can't be satisfied. Got the Weary
had died.""I got the Weary Blue And I can't be satisfie
d I wish that I had died.""I got the Weary Blue And I
n't happy no mo' And I wish that I had died.""I got the
satisfied— I ain't happy no mo' And I wish that I had
ues And can't be satisfied— I ain't happy no mo' And I w
t the Weary Blues And can't be satisfied— I ain't happy
got the Weary Blue And I can't be satisfied. Got the W
at I had died.""I got the Weary Blue And I can't be sat
And I wish that I had died.""I got the Weary Blue And
n't happy no mo' And I wish that I had died.""I got the
satisfied— I ain't happy no mo' And I wish that I had
ues And can't be satisfied— I ain't happy no mo' And I w
t the Weary Blues And can't be satisfied— I ain't happy
satisfied. Got the Weary Blues And can't be satisfied—
ue And I can't be satisfied. Got the Weary Blues And ca
t the Weary Blue And I can't be satisfied. Got the Weary
had died.""I got the Weary Blue And I can't be satisfie
d I wish that I had died.""I got the Weary Blue And I
n't happy no mo' And I wish that I had died.""I got the
satisfied— I ain't happy no mo' And I wish that I had
ues And can't be satisfied— I ain't happy no mo' And I w
t the Weary Blues And can't be satisfied— I ain't happy
satisfied. Got the Weary Blues And can't be satisfied—
ue And I can't be satisfied. Got the Weary Blues And ca
t the Weary Blue And I can't be satisfied. Got the Weary

Part I:
The Life of
Langston Hughes

LANGSTON HUGHES IS SHOWN AS A BABY, HELD BY HIS MOTHER, CARRIE.

Chapter 1

A Blues Life

Joplin, Missouri, was a booming town in 1900. The thriving city, situated near the southwestern border of the state, profited hugely from a mining and prospecting industry that found southwest Missouri a veritable treasure trove of natural minerals. By the time Langston Hughes was born in Joplin in 1902, that city had become the lead and zinc capital of the world—a place where a loaf of bread would hardly have cost four cents, a gallon of milk twenty-eight cents, and an automobile, a new luxury item, more than nine hundred dollars. Hughes's father, James Nathaniel Hughes, took a job as a stenographer for the Lincoln Mining Company, earning a modest twenty-five dollars per month, just enough to keep his new wife comfortable in a rented cottage residence at 1602 Missouri Avenue in Joplin.

James Hughes and Carrie Langston married on April 30, 1899, in Guthrie, Oklahoma, a few short miles from the black township that bore Carrie Langston's family name. Like Guthrie, where James and Carrie met, Langston, Oklahoma, attracted African-American settlers, farmers, cowboys, and speculators by the thousands. They were lured by talk of land grabs, new business opportunities, and the prospects of many all-black townships being founded nearby. Not yet admitted into statehood, the Oklahoma territory was an exciting draw for James Hughes, an ambitious African-American schoolteacher, farmer, grocer, and law clerk from Charlestown, Indiana. Despite Oklahoma's appeal for African Americans at the turn of the century and its relative racial freedoms, its enduring racism did not allow James Hughes to fulfill his most ardent ambition: to practice law in the Oklahoma territory. He would soon leave Oklahoma and settle in Joplin, Missouri.

For all its industrial wealth, however, Joplin, too, would prove to be insufficiently rewarding for a man with big ambitions who detested nothing more sternly than black indigence (so sternly that he took to despising even the black poor themselves). In 1901, after two years of work and marriage in Joplin, James and Carrie set out for Buffalo, New York. Little is known about why they chose to relocate to Buffalo, but it was there, less than six months later, that Carrie discovered she was pregnant. Already, though, James was intent upon moving to Cuba, whatever the sacrifice, for a business venture. By year's end, he \had settled alone in Cuba. Either unwilling or physically unable to follow her husband so far from home, Carrie returned to Joplin, where she delivered a son on February 1, 1902, two months after her separation from James. Still, Carrie named her newborn after his distant father. James Langston Hughes was his proper name. Soon enough, however, James was dropped in favor of Langston, a name of mark made prominent by Carrie's uncle John Mercer Langston, an extraordinary lawyer, professor, statesman, abolitionist, and the first African American elected to Congress in Virginia. Against this complicated background of proud ancestry and an absent father, Langston Hughes entered the world at the dawn of the twentieth century.

Childhood

At Hughes's birth, his young mother found herself alone in Joplin with an infant son to care for and unfulfilled dreams of becoming a theater actor and performer. Resentful and wounded, Hughes's mother did not take joyfully to motherhood, it seems, and, although she was present, did not take an active part in his upbringing. Instead, it was Hughes's grandmother, Mary Langston, who took upon herself the primary responsibility of caring for young Hughes while his mother worked and lodged elsewhere, usually out of town. With occasional help from Carrie, and with James Hughes entirely divorced from his son's rearing, Mary Langston, approaching seventy years old when Hughes was born, raised her grandson until her death when he was twelve.

Naturally, her influence upon Hughes was deep. Moving him with her from Joplin back to her home in Lawrence, Kansas, when Hughes was not much more than a toddler, she stirred him with her gift of storytelling. Sitting at the foot of her rocker, Hughes delighted in Mary's stories of slavery and freedom, proud family heritage, and adventure and heroism. In her stories were lessons of black American pride and valor that Hughes would soon need to comfort and reassure him when the ugly face of racism caused him to doubt his own intelligence and talents. More than once did the "dreamy little boy" (Rampersad, 1.13) have to fight back feelings of racial inferiority caused by the insult of others' racial prejudice.

When Hughes entered the Pinckney School in Lawrence as a second grader, he was assigned to a single segregated classroom along with the school's other black children, first through third graders. Because of Lawrence's segregation laws (dubbed Jim Crow laws all over the country), none of the city's black children were permitted to swim at the local YMCA or register in the Boy Scouts as they might have liked. When the Patee Theater on Massachusetts Street suddenly reversed its policy of admitting "colored" people, posting a new sign prohibiting African Americans from entering, it was a blow to young Hughes's pride. It left him a wounded eight-year-old incapable of making any sense at all of the adult absurdity of racial discrimination or the juvenile name-calling by white kids who belittled him as a "ni--er" on more than a couple of occasions. What was left for him but to internalize those gloomy feelings of inferiority that race prejudice tends to produce in fragile black children? To add insult to injury, Hughes's grandmother was not at all well off. Although she kept Hughes's clothes clean and neatly pressed, he was often ashamed of her sacrifice to keep him appearing that way: her own clothes were the worn-down, secondhand giveaways of neighborhood women who respected her matronly resolve to clothe and feed Hughes, but saw how difficult it was for a woman her age, unable to work, to do so. Hughes's peers taunted him cruelly about his grandmother's age and appearance, and he was frequently humiliated by their poverty. Mary Langston—so needy that she soon moved the two of them out of her house at 732 Alabama Street in order to rent it out for income—tried mightily to protect her grandson from all the insults of segregation and poverty. Unfortunately, she could not shield him from all suffering. But what embarrassments she could not protect him from, she made up for by exposing him to a wealth of culture and inspiration for which little money was needed.

With grandmother Mary, Hughes sat amid a great crowd of locals gathered to hear a speech by the best-known African American of his era: the matchless orator, Booker T. Washington. And not many boys his age, black or white, ever got the chance to see and hear former president Theodore Roosevelt up close and personal as Hughes did. Hughes's grandmother was the widow of one of abolitionist John Brown's twenty-one coconspirators. At the dedication of the John Brown Memorial Battlefield in Osawatomie, Kansas, a short sixty miles from Lawrence, she had been a guest of honor. Seated alongside Mary Langston, the impressionable eight-year-old knew only that something was extraordinary and historical about the event and the nobility of the former president's speechmaking just a few feet away from his own seat on the dais. These were monumental moments for the sensitive little boy.

Still, life in Lawrence was extremely lonely for Hughes, despite Mary Langston's heroic efforts to give him a happy childhood. His loneliness would lead him to discover the wonderful world of books, a world his mother had introduced to him years earlier in one of Topeka's quiet vine-covered public libraries. From the start young Hughes read voraciously. He regularly read black periodicals such as the *Chicago Defender* newspaper and the *Crisis* magazine. Classic American novels like Harriet Beecher Stowe's *Uncle Tom's Cabin* and Mark Twain's *Adventures of Huckleberry Finn* kept him delightfully engrossed in their pages. And Paul Lawrence Dunbar, "the true fireside poet of the black American home" (Rampersad, 1.19) was an early poetry favorite. These works, along with the Bible, were the most important written works in shaping Hughes into the young grammar-school poet he would soon become.

From Lawrence to Lincoln

Although life in Lawrence, Kansas, was lonesome for a boy who was almost thirteen, it was comfortable and secure just the same. The sudden passing of Hughes's seventy-nine-year-old grandmother, however, quickly changed everything. Hughes entered the eighth grade not in Lawrence but in the small hamlet of Lincoln, Illinois, with its population of 12,000 residents. There, he joined his mother, Carrie, her new husband, a former cook named Homer Clark, and a two-year-old stepbrother, Gwyn Shannon Clark. Although Hughes and his new, refashioned family did not live in Lincoln long enough for Hughes to begin high school there, the several months he spent there were especially memorable ones for him. The experience of traditional family life with a mother, father, and brother was a world apart from the more lonesome one he knew with his grandmother. It was also in Lincoln that Hughes composed and gave a public reading of his first poem, a sixteen-line tribute to the teachers and

HUGHES STANDS WITH HIS GRANDMOTHER, HIS STEPFATHER HOMER CLARK, AND HIS STEPBROTHER AND MOTHER OUTSIDE THEIR HOME.

students at Lincoln's Central School where Hughes held the honored title of eighth-grade class poet. The enormous respect he gained from his teachers and classmates at Central transformed Hughes. "It had never occurred to me to be a poet before," he recalled later on (*Big Sea*, 24). But his teachers' and peers' adulation of his poetry at the end-of-the-year graduation exercises sealed, in his own mind, an unquestionable poetic future. Lincoln was a short-lived, but extraordinarily significant episode in the young life of a talent who would ultimately mature to the place of black America's greatest poet ever.

Finding Poetry at Central High

At the end of the summer of 1916, Hughes found himself uprooted again and off—with Carrie, Homer, and Gwyn—to Cleveland, Ohio, where Homer, unable to find good work in Lincoln, had already gone for work in a local steel mill. In Cleveland the family settled into a basement apartment. Unfortunately, prejudiced white landlords charged African Americans more than double the rent that their white tenants paid. Homer and Carrie had little choice but to pay the ridiculous rent that was being demanded for their tiny apartment. To help make the rent, Carrie took on work as a maid. The weight of the family's financial hardships grew heavier, though, when Homer was forced to quit his job at the steel mill. The heat of the mill's furnaces and the dangerously strenuous labor his job required all but ruined Homer's health.

For Hughes, school was a refuge from the unpleasant conditions of the mills where he might have had to find work otherwise, and from his family's cold, compact apartment. Fortunately for Hughes, Cleveland's historic

HUGHES STANDS ALONE IN THE SNOW, AND WITH THREE FRIENDS, IN THESE PHOTOS SHOT OUTSIDE CENTRAL HIGH SCHOOL IN CLEVELAND, OHIO.

Central High School was one of the best in the city, counting among its storied graduates the likes of oil tycoon John D. Rockefeller. By the time of Hughes's enrollment, Central's student body was a significantly diverse one. The majority of students were children and grandchildren of Cleveland's European immigrants, since Cleveland's wealthy white population had withdrawn from the city to resettle in the suburbs. Some African-American students also attended Central, but their numbers were far from evidencing that black students were an integral part of the rich diversity of Central's students. Despite this, Hughes was at ease there. As a freshman he succeeded brilliantly in school, excelling in graphic art, and he soon distinguished himself as a budding poet. The next year he made Central's track team, but it was in his poetry, which was getting to be more and more of a serious activity, that a greater vigor was coming into view.

In the spring of 1918, Hughes began publishing his first serious verses in the school magazine, the Central High *Monthly*. Before summer the student editors of the *Monthly* had accepted six of his poems. Returning to Central in the fall after a miserable summer break spent in South Chicago visiting Carrie—separated from Homer again—and Gwyn, Hughes joined *Monthly*'s editorial staff. A few months later he became editor in chief of an independent section of the *Monthly* called the "Belfry Owl." In those days, Hughes recalled writing about "love, about the steel mills where my step-father worked," and "the slums where we lived and the brown girls from the South, prancing up and down Central Avenue on a spring day" (*The Big Sea*, 28). Modeling his verses after his favorite boyhood poets, Paul Lawrence Dunbar and Carl Sandburg, many of Hughes's early verses were either "little Negro dialect poems" like Dunbar's, or free-verse poems like Sandburg's. Emulating Dunbar, one high school poem went:

Just because I loves you—
That's de reason why
My soul is full of color
Like de wings of a butterfly.

Just because I loves you
That's de reason why
My heart's a fluttering aspen leaf
When you pass by. (*The Big Sea*, 28–29)

Sandburg, however, was Hughes's "guiding star." Taking Sandburg as a model and, very probably, a broken Homer Clark for his inspiration, Hughes wrote of the steel mills:

The mills
That grind and grind,
That grind out steel
And grind away the lives
Of men—
In the sunset their stacks
Are great black silhouettes
Against the sky.
In the dawn
They belch red fire.
The mills—
Grinding out new steel,
Old men. (*The Big Sea*, 29)

By the end of his sophomore year at Central, Hughes had become a serious writer.

Hughes's junior and senior years at Central were thrilling. He was voted class poet and became editor of the school yearbook. The track relay team repeated as city champions, and he was reelected to the student council. At the encouragement of his friend, Sartur Andrzejewski, the son of Polish immigrants, Hughes performed in more than one school play. Soon graduation was upon him. With his friends going off to college, some to Cleveland's premier Western Reserve University and others to Columbia University in New York, Hughes had some tough decisions to make. He could not afford college. So, swallowing his pride and suppressing a deep resentment for his father that he had developed over the years, Hughes went reluctantly to see him. His father was living in Mexico after his failed venture in Cuba and was employed by the American-owned Sultepec Electric Light and Power Company in Mexico City. Hughes hoped his father would pay the tuition to Columbia University.

On the train to Mexico, just outside of St. Louis, Hughes wrote one of his best-known poems ever. "The Negro Speaks of Rivers" was the first of his publications to appear in a national magazine, the *Crisis*, and a poetic tribute to the eternal strength and steadfastness of the African-American people whom he loved (and whom his father, though black himself, seemed to hate):

I've known rivers:
I've known rivers ancient as the world and older than the flow of human blood in human veins.

My soul has grown deep like the rivers.

I bathed in the Euphrates when dawns were young.
I built my hut near the Congo and it lulled me to sleep.
I looked upon the Nile and raised the pyramids above it.
I heard the singing of the Mississippi when Abe Lincoln went down to New Orleans, and I've seen its muddy bosom turn all golden in the sunset.

I've known rivers:
Ancient, dusky rivers.
My soul has grown deep like the rivers.
(*Collected Poems*, 23)

Not coincidentally, Hughes had a brilliant view of the muddy Mississippi River out of the train's window. Despite his hesitations about making the trip, Hughes's journey south was perfectly poetic.

Summer in Mexico

The good feeling Hughes and his father first shared when Hughes arrived in Mexico turned sour as soon as James made it clear that he did not plan to pay his son's college tuition. Instead, James proposed that Hughes study abroad in Switzerland and Germany. There, in James's vision, Hughes would learn engineering before returning to Mexico to settle down (probably close to James) as a mining engineer. The idea disappointed Hughes. He did not want to become an engineer. His own dream, he told his father, was to become a writer. "A writer?" James asked in disbelief, "Do they make any money?" (Rampersad, 1.43). Writing might be a satisfying hobby, James meant to imply, but no writer he ever heard of— especially no black writer—had earned a living by it. His father's discouragement deeply dismayed Hughes, but it was not enough to bury his hopes of one day becoming a successful writer.

That summer passed uneventfully. Mostly, Hughes read books, rode horses, feasted on apple cakes, and wrote poems. Although these pastimes were satisfying enough for Hughes, his father's unbending stubbornness helped him understand what frustrated his mother so much about his father. He also realized how steadfastly his grandmother, whom he missed terribly, encouraged his dreams. In the voice of a brave black mother much like his own (or Mary Langston's), he wrote:

Well, son, I'll tell you:
Life for me ain't been no crystal stair.
It's had tacks in it,
And splinters,
And boards torn up,
And places with no carpet on the floor—
Bare.
But all the time
I'se been a-climbin' on,
And reachin' landin's,
And turnin' corners,
And sometimes goin' in the dark
Where there ain't been no light.
So boy, don't you turn back.

Then, as if having this humble mother give the advice he needed so much for himself, the poet went on:

Don't you set down on the steps,
'Cause you find it's kinder hard.
Don't you fall now—
For I'se still goin', honey,
I'se still climbin',
And life for me ain't been no crystal stair.
("Mother to Son," *Collected Poems*, 30)

Pining for his mother and dreaming of Harlem in New York, "the greatest Negro city in the world" (*Big Sea*, 62), and nearby Columbia University, Hughes nevertheless passed nearly a year in Mexico, happily distracted teaching English to the locals and taking in the weekly bullfights. Before his second summer there had ended, Hughes succeeded in getting a few of his poems and a children's play published, the first fruits of the influential writing career that was to come. Seeing Hughes's success, and the pure delight of his achievement, James finally relented and agreed to send Hughes to Columbia University.

Columbia and Harlem

New York, with its great towers rising up out of the magenta sunset "growing slowly taller and taller" above the water "until they looked as if they could almost touch the sky" (*Big Sea*, 80), was immediately enthralling. And Harlem, with all its noise, speed, and beautiful black people, took Hughes's breath away. Columbia, he learned, was just a few blocks south of 125th Street, the center of Harlem.

Almost immediately, Hughes discovered he didn't like Columbia. It was Harlem, not college, which fascinated him. The campus was all cold and stone buildings. Because he was "colored," he had no small difficulty getting a dorm room. Though one had been assigned to him when he was accepted, it was revoked when he got to school. Apparently, the housing office at Columbia assumed, because his application had been sent from his father's residence with no hint of his race, that Hughes was Mexican. Though Columbia generously accommodated its foreign students, black students (there were only twelve or so) were barred from living in the campus dormitories. One of the wealthiest colleges anywhere, Columbia was far too exclusive to grant African Americans the social equality of whites that would have been made evident by their living together in the dormitories. Presumably, Columbia's white students and alumni would not have tolerated a racially integrated housing policy. Desperate for a place on campus, and with nothing at all to lose, Hughes protested. Finally, after considerable persistence on the part of Hughes, the housing office gave in and granted him a cold room near a noisy entrance in one of its high-rise dormitories.

The rest of the year went no better. Hughes made few friends at rich Columbia. His classes bored him terribly.

Cruelly, the school newspaper gave him assignments impossible for an African-American student—barred from the fraternity houses and high-society events the paper wanted him to cover—to fill. Only the allure of Harlem, a mecca of black artists, actors, musicians, and race leaders, kept Hughes happy about coming to New York. Soon, it would attract his mother, too. Although they were just as poor in New York as they had been in Cleveland, Hughes and Carrie shared a love for Harlem. There they met some of the most important African Americans of their day, including the most influential race leader and writer of the twentieth century, W. E. B. DuBois, the famous black woman writer Jessie Fauset, and the celebrated poet-musician-diplomat, James Weldon Johnson. To Hughes, especially, Harlem was almost heavenly.

At the beginning of his second school term in 1922, Hughes began planning his move out of the dormitory and into his own place in Harlem. His grades at Columbia were good, but a new life in Harlem was calling. He attended public lectures at the Harlem Branch Library on 135th Street and listened to Harlem's great poets, Claude McKay and Eric Walrond, read from their works. Inspired by Harlem's colorful days and dimly lit, jazz-rich nights, Hughes wrote more new poems now than ever. Several were also published. Under a pen name, he published a version of his black dialect poem, "Just Because I Loves You," one of his Central High works, in the Columbia *Spectator* magazine. *Crisis* magazine, published by DuBois and the National Association for the Advancement of Colored People (NAACP), printed two of his works, "My Loves" and "To a Dead Friend," as they had "The Negro Speaks of Rivers" a couple of years earlier. A paper in Berlin, Germany, even reprinted one of Hughes's poems during the months he was getting better acquainted with Harlem. At last, in May Hughes made two important decisions. First, though his father had recently suffered a stroke and was very ill as a result, Hughes had no plans to return to Mexico. Second, he decided he would not return to Columbia in the fall. The next several months were not at all easy for Hughes. With no more support coming from his father in Mexico, and his mother gone back to Cleveland, money was getting ever more difficult to come by. Racial prejudice was making it next to impossible for Hughes, or any other African-American man, to make a living in New York in 1922. Very few job ads welcomed "colored boys" to apply. Finally, Hughes found work miles outside of Manhattan on Staten Island. The work was tough, but exhilarating just the same. A stranger to farming, Hughes found himself, for the first time in his life, living off the land, "ploughing, hoeing, spreading manure, picking weeds, washing lettuce, beets, carrots, onions, tying them and packing them for market, loading the wagons" (*The Big Sea*, 86). All of this Hughes did for fifty dollars per month, including bed and board. It was demanding work, and his bed was only a pile of hay in the corner of a barn, but Hughes liked it for the most part. And what small details he didn't like, he endured. He knew that living and working on that farm on Staten Island probably saved his life.

The Big Sea
At the end of the harvesting season, Hughes had saved enough money to return to Harlem to purchase an overcoat for the upcoming winter and to rent a room in a boardinghouse. He found work for a short time delivering flowers, but, with a disagreeable shop owner for a boss who reminded him of his father, Hughes found the job unbearable. Early one morning he walked straight away from his duties at Thorley's flower shop and out to the South Street wharves, looking for a freighter to take him far away from the day-to-day difficulties of earning a living in New York. If a lifetime of earning impossibly low wages

was to be his fate, Hughes reasoned, he might as well see the world while he worked for them.

At the U.S. Shipping Board office, Hughes discovered that there was an opening for a menial hand onboard one of the client ships. Without so much as asking where in the world his ship was headed, he took the job immediately. Instead of heading out into the wide ocean, though, Hughes found himself headed up the Hudson River to Jones Point, New York, not far from the more famous West Point. That winter, perfectly isolated at Jones Point among the more than one hundred ships indefinitely anchored there, Hughes penned the first of what was to become a new type of poetry, modern and almost musical, that he would make famous and continue to write for the rest of his career: the blues poem. With "The Weary Blues," Hughes captured the mood and rhythms of the early blues he heard as a kid in Kansas, where the blues had thrived like nowhere else:

> Droning a drowsy syncopated tune,
> Rocking back and forth to a mellow croon,
> I heard a Negro play.
> Down on Lenox Avenue the other night
> By the pale dull pallor of an old gas light
> He did a lazy sway. . . .
> He did a lazy sway. . . .
> To the tune o' those Weary Blues.
> With his ebony hands on each ivory key
> He made that poor piano moan with melody.
> O Blues!
> Swaying to and fro on his rickety stool
> He played that sad raggy tune like a musical fool.
> Sweet Blues!
> Coming from a black man's soul.
> O Blues!
> In a deep song voice with a melancholy tone
> I heard that Negro sing, the old piano moan—

"Ain't got nobody in all this world,
Ain't got nobody but ma self.
I's gwine to quit ma frownin'
And put ma troubles on the shelf."
Thump, thump, thump, went his foot on the floor.
He played a few chords then he sang some more—
"I got the Weary Blues
And I can't be satisfied.
Got the Weary Blues
And can't be satisfied—
I ain't happy no mo'
And I wish that I had died."
And far into the night he crooned that tune.
The stars went out and so did the moon.
The singer stopped playing and went to bed
While the Weary Blues echoed through his head.
He slept like a rock or a man that's dead.
(*Collected Poems*, 50)

Considered his best work since "The Negro Speaks of Rivers," "The Weary Blues" turned a lowly black music form, the blues, into respectable poetry. The poem honored the blues and all the nameless blues artists whose music was so closely associated with the everyday black people Hughes loved so much.

When the spring came he decided to take leave of the fleet of old ships docked in upstate New York in hopes of finding a ship that was really going somewhere. His hopes were soon realized, and young Hughes, still a lowly hand, joined a crew of seamen headed for Africa. The trip took six months. Once landed on the long, sandy African coastline, bright with gleaming palm trees, the *West Hesseltine* unloaded its cargo of industrial machinery, boxes of tools, crates of canned goods, and a number of popular Hollywood films. In return, a crew of men of the Kru tribe loaded the weather-worn vessel with a treasure trove of palm oil, cocoa beans, and ton-sized mahogany logs.

For the first time, Hughes had come face-to-face with native Africans. He tried meeting them on the common ground of their shared race and heritage, but his attempt was laughed at. To the Africans, Hughes was not black like them. Although his skin was a clear copper-brown, the Africans he met declared: "You, white man! You, white man!" To these Africans, since Hughes's complexion was not deep black like their own, and he appeared more like a man of mixed races, he was not *black* the way they were. Hughes was, in practical terms, *white*. He protested that he was not white. The Africans coldly insisted he was not black, either. Oddly, Africa was the only place in the world Hughes was not regarded a black man.

Despite the shock of being called a white man by the Africans, with whom he believed he shared a common ancestry, Hughes remained confident that, like it or not, he was indeed black. He composed the poem "Dream Variation" to help him make his case:

To fling my arms wide
In some place of the sun,
To whirl and to dance
Till the white day is done.
Then rest at cool evening
Beneath a tall tree
While night comes on gently,
Dark like me,—
That is my dream!

To fling my arms wide
In the face of the sun,
Dance! Whirl! Whirl!
Till the quick day is done.
Rest at pale evening . . .
A tall, slim tree . . .
Night coming tenderly
Black like me. (*Collected Poems*, 40)

In all, the *West Hesseltine* ship docked at thirty-two ports, including Senegal, the Ivory Coast, the Gold Coast, Congo, Benin, and Angola. Every stop offered a different picture of the colorful beauty of Africa. After six months at sea, through good and bad weather, the *West Hesseltine* headed back to America. On an early autumn morning, it docked in Brooklyn. Hughes disembarked with high spirits and headed for Harlem.

Harlem was hopping and hotter than ever. The 135th Street library was now hosting public lectures and readings regularly. New young African-American writers were coming to Harlem in increasing numbers. Jean Toomer, who dazzled the literary world with his brilliant modern work, *Cane*, only a year earlier, Gwendolyn Bennett, and the short-story writer Eric Walrond each made considerable splashes of their own. Still, Hughes needed work, and before long, he was looking again to the sea. This time Hughes signed up for a bigger, cleaner freighter, the *McKeesport*, leaving out of Hoboken, New Jersey, on its way to Rotterdam, Holland. In Rotterdam Hughes took his pay, twenty-five dollars, got off the ship, and caught the train to Paris.

In Paris Hughes took a position as a dishwasher at the famed Le Grand Duc jazz club for a salary of fifteen francs per night and breakfast. Happily, the experience of Le Grand Duc inspired more poetry. The swing-time and jazz rhythms he heard there every night seeped into his verse:

"Me an' ma baby's
Got two mo' ways,
Two mo' ways to do de Charleston!"
Da, da,
Da, da da!
Two mo' ways to do de Charleston!"
("Negro Dancers," *Collected Poems*, 44)

In Paris, Hughes's circle of friends suddenly widened. Alain Locke, a philosophy professor from Howard University in Washington, D.C., was passing through Paris and paid Hughes a visit. They talked poetry and art, took a stroll in the park, and attended an opera together. Locke hoped to convince Hughes to return stateside and finish college. Only he was not thinking of Columbia. Locke had his own Howard University in mind. The idea of attending the historically black college intrigued Hughes, and he agreed to it. In the meantime, Locke introduced him to Albert Barnes, the Pennsylvanian owner of one of the finest collections of modern art anywhere, and to Paul Guillaume, a Frenchman with a renowned collection of African art. Soon Hughes found himself in the company of such distinguished men as René Maran, the celebrated Martiniquan writer, and Prince Kojo Touvalou Houènou of Dahomey. After Paris, Hughes landed in Italy, taking in Genoa and Venice and as many of their palaces, churches, monuments, and paintings as he could before sailing aboard the *West Cawthon* back across the Atlantic to America. How incredible it was for a humble dishwasher and amateur poet from small-town Kansas to find himself in equal fellowship with such renowned men.

Seventh Street, Washington, D.C.

Back in America, Hughes returned to Harlem long enough to attend a benefit cabaret party at Happy Rhone's Club on Harlem's Lenox Avenue. All of Harlem's important people were there. Writers DuBois, Johnson, and Carl Van Vechten, and entertainers like Florence Mills, Noble Sissle, and Bill "Bojangles" Robinson all greeted him like a younger brother. Harlem was abuzz about Hughes's homecoming. A steady stream of the young writer's work had made the pages of some prominent journals while he was abroad. People were eager to meet the rising star, and Hughes was all too happy to oblige them. He was as thrilled about the new energy of Harlem he was coming home to as he had ever been. However, his excitement about Harlem couldn't kill his curiosity about Washington, D.C.

TO MAKE MONEY, LANGSTON HUGHES WORKED AS A BUSBOY AT THE WARDMAN HOTEL IN WASHINGTON, D.C. IT WAS DURING THIS TIME THAT HUGHES WAS FIRST RECOGNIZED AS A POET.

Hughes had read a good deal about Washington. It was said to be a fine place for black society. Hughes had hoped to live in Washington, in fact, among the city's refined black citizens. In the waning days of 1924, Hughes moved into the home of a few well-to-do relatives in Washington's LeDroit Park district. They were descendents of his esteemed great-uncle, John Mercer Langston, and very well-known among Washington's black elites. Their prominence was not altogether extraordinary, however. On their block was a much-admired Methodist bishop, a judge, a high-ranking government employee, two physicians, attorneys, a university administrator, and an architect. Although significant numbers of noteworthy figures lived in Harlem, too, they were mostly artists like Hughes, whose considerable stature nevertheless guaranteed nothing of the wealth enjoyed by the Washington elites. It seemed that nowhere had more well-to-do African Americans than Washington.

For a while, Hughes tried hard to get on with the society folks in Washington. To keep up appearances, he tried working as a page at the Library of Congress, and then as a newspaperman for the *Sentinel*, Washington's black weekly. A series of lesser jobs followed when Hughes quit the *Sentinel* after concluding the paper was not interested in his writing at all. It was interested only in his selling advertising space. Ultimately, however, Hughes got lucky. He found work that promised the sort of pay and prestige that contented sophisticated black Washingtonians. For the next several months until he left Washington, Hughes was a clerk, research assistant, and office boy for the preeminent black historian, Carter G. Woodson. Woodson, educated at the University of Chicago and Harvard and the first proponent of Negro History Week (which would evolve over several decades into African American History Month), was an extraordinary scholar. Editor of the influential *Journal of Negro History* and one of the founding members of the Association for the Study of Negro Life and History in 1916, Woodson put Hughes to work dusting, polishing, sorting and answering mail, preparing publications, and occasionally overseeing the staff.

Woodson required a lot of Hughes, perhaps seeing the younger man's promise and wanting to help teach him about high standards and self-discipline. Hughes valued his work for Woodson, and Woodson's project, *Free Negro Heads of Families in the United States in 1830*, even more. It was "a fine contribution," Hughes would say, "to the Negro people and to America" (quoted in Rampersad, 1.101). As Woodson's assistant, Hughes played an important role in the older scholar's project.

As hard as Hughes tried to keep up the appearance of belonging to the high-class inhabitants of LeDroit Park, he found the Seventh Street section of Washington less stiff and more to his liking. There, plain, everyday black people from the South lived. Hughes enjoyed the plainness of their lives, their jazz and their blues, and their storefront church services. On Seventh Street the people were down to earth. They lived rough lives. Hughes learned a lot about the meaning of the blues by observing the city's poor black citizens. Many of the poems Hughes wrote during the fourteen months he spent living in Washington were inspired by the blues he heard there, and it was an important period of Hughes's growth as a poet. In journals and magazines of many kinds, he published more poems in this period than he ever did before. One poem he called "Cross":

My old man's a white old man
And my old mother's black.
If ever I cursed my white old man
I take my curses back.

If ever I cursed my black old mother
And wished she were in hell,
I'm sorry for that evil wish
And now I wish her well.

My old man died in a fine big house
My ma died in a shack.
I wonder where I am going to die,
Being neither white nor black? (*Collected Poems*, 58–59)

Just as important as the education he received from observing the lives of some of Washington's poorest citizens, the success of a new collection of poems, short stories, essays, and drama assembled by Professor Locke made a great impression on Hughes's career. Locke's book, *The New Negro*, created a stir, and Hughes's fame, and the fame of many of his writer friends in New York, grew because of it. But Hughes did not always welcome fame. Not long after *The New Negro* was published, a local Washington book club organized a dinner to honor Hughes and his friends. The dinner was formal, but Hughes did not own a formal jacket and tie to wear. His mother, who was also invited, did not own formal clothes either. After discussing the problem at length, the club permitted Hughes to attend the dinner in his best clothes, even though they were not the formal attire the club expected. His mother would have to stay home, though. Without formal attire, she was not welcome. The book club's decision was an insult. Hughes was so angry that his mother was not welcome at the dinner that he refused to attend himself.

Not everyone in Washington was as rude as the members of the book club. Hughes would soon meet a kind woman named Georgia Douglas Johnson who opened her home every Saturday evening to young writers for poetry readings and good company. Johnson's home was very popular with Washington's young artists. She served cake and wine at every Saturday gathering and welcomed young writers like Hughes into her group of friends. For Hughes, Johnson was like a breath of fresh air in Washington. Through her, Hughes met other important black writers, including Rudolph Fisher, Marita Bonner, and Angelina Grimké.

One of the most exciting subjects of conversation at Johnson's home was a recently announced literary contest. Almost all of the young writers who came to Johnson's home each week submitted something to the contest. Hughes turned in several poems, including his much-admired "The Weary Blues." When the judging was over, Hughes had won first prize! An awards banquet was held in New York, and the great poet James Weldon Johnson recited Hughes's "The Weary Blues" to the banquet crowd. After the ceremony, Hughes mingled with other new black writers who had come to the banquet from all over the United States. It was at this New York banquet that Hughes first met the very funny and somewhat oddball writer Zora

Neale Hurston from Florida. She was an eccentric figure who could be found on the streets of Harlem, for example, completely at ease soliciting strangers to measure their heads for anthropology research. Hughes liked her right away and they became fast friends.

Carl Van Vechten was also in the crowd. Van Vechten, a white man, knew all of the most famous African Americans in New York and helped to support their work financially. Van Vechten enjoyed deep friendships with James Weldon Johnson, Paul Robeson, the black actor and singer, and A'Lelia Walker, heiress to the Madame C. J. Walker hair care fortune (Madame C. J. Walker was the country's first self-made black female millionaire). Decidedly well off and devoted to African-American art, music, literature, and theater, Van Vechten admired Hughes instantly. His respect paid off almost immediately. Less than a month after the banquet, a letter arrived at Hughes's Washington apartment from the publishing house of Alfred Knopf. Van Vechten had shown some of Hughes's poems to this major New York publisher and had encouraged Knopf to make a book of poems out of them. Knopf agreed that Hughes's poems were beautiful and wrote to Hughes to say so. In the envelope with a letter of compliments for Hughes's poems was also a book contract for Hughes to sign and return. With mounting fame and a book of poetry soon to come out, Hughes was on his way from an up-and-coming young writer to becoming a major black poet. He would give his book the same title as his prize-winning poem, *The Weary Blues*. It was 1925. Hughes was twenty-three years old.

With *The Weary Blues* soon to be published, Hughes wanted publicity. In November, he had his chance. Vachel Lindsay, one of America's best-known poets, was a guest at the Washington hotel where Hughes was a new busboy. Recognizing Lindsay from his picture in the morning newspaper, Hughes copied down three of his poems and slipped them onto the hotel dinner table where Lindsay was dining. It was a sly but important move. Later that night, at a public reading of his own works, Lindsay announced the discovery of a new poet, a black poet, who was working as a busboy at Washington's Wardman Hotel. Lindsay then read to his large white audience all three of the poems Hughes slipped to him. The next day news reporters found Hughes at the Wardman. They asked him about his unique talents, and Hughes was more than happy to answer their questions. Lindsay's "discovery" of Hughes made not only the local but the national press. It was a grand moment for Hughes. The only disappointment was that Lindsay was not free to meet him, since more readings and other business required him to leave right away. No matter. Hughes had his big break. No longer an emerging talent known only by the Harlem types, he was now becoming a nationally recognized writer.

Lincoln

In the months just before *The Weary Blues* landed on the shelves of libraries and book stalls, Hughes decided to take a second crack at college. Not at Howard, as he first planned, but at Lincoln University in Pennsylvania. Sometimes called "The black Princeton," Lincoln University pleased Hughes immediately. For the first time since third grade, he belonged to an entirely black student body. He loved being among his own people. An all-male college and seminary founded by religious abolitionists for the education of newly freed slaves, Lincoln enjoyed a significant reputation, but its students were largely poor, and its alumni were not as moneyed as those who supported Columbia. Although it struck Hughes as "wonderful," it was hardly paradise. The buildings were in disrepair. The library was sadly lacking books, and the dorms and dining hall were overcrowded. The dullness of a required Bible class tested the students' perseverance. But the Lincoln students, all three hundred of them, took pride in "dear old Lincoln" just the same. Hughes took to Lincoln warmly.

HUGHES WAS HAPPY ONCE HE GOT TO LINCOLN
UNIVERSITY IN PENNSYLVANIA, HIS SECOND STAB AT BEING
A COLLEGE STUDENT.

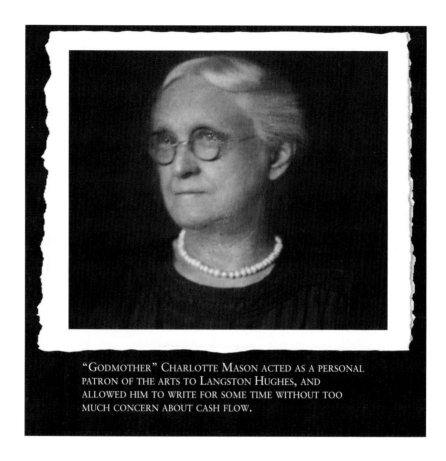

"GODMOTHER" CHARLOTTE MASON ACTED AS A PERSONAL PATRON OF THE ARTS TO LANGSTON HUGHES, AND ALLOWED HIM TO WRITE FOR SOME TIME WITHOUT TOO MUCH CONCERN ABOUT CASH FLOW.

Near the end of the term, Hughes took on a new challenge. An essay by George Schuyler called "The Negro-Art Hokum" came to him by mail. The essay, sent to him by the editor of *Nation* magazine, poked fun at the idea of a separate black artistic tradition like the one Hughes's friend, Alain Locke, wrote of in the introduction of *The New Negro.* Hughes disagreed strongly with Schuyler's views and wrote an essay of his own in rebuttal, just as the *Nation* hoped. His response to Schuyler, "The Negro Artist and the Racial Mountain," turned out to be perhaps the most important (and to his generation of artists, inspiring) essay of his life. In it, Hughes wrote of how sad it was that some black poets were so ashamed of black culture that they wanted nothing to do with writing poetry about black people or their lives. But Hughes saw in black people a treasure trove of material for an exciting new black poetry, especially by younger black poets. "We younger Negro artists who create now," he proclaimed, "intend to express our individual dark-skinned selves without fear or shame." And he continued:

> If white people are pleased we are glad. If they are not, it doesn't matter. We know we are beautiful. And ugly too. The tom-tom cries and the tom-tom laughs. If colored people are pleased we are glad. If they are not, their displeasure doesn't matter either. We build our temples for tomorrow, strong as we know how, and we stand on top of the mountain, free within ourselves. (Huggins, *Voices*, 309)

Hughes's essay made a strong statement to the world. It would soon rally together young black artists and inspire a movement of black poetry, art, theater, novels, and music called the Harlem Renaissance. Writing more essays and winning more poetry contests, Hughes was one of the movement's leading voices. Other major writers and visual artists of the movement included Zora Neale Hurston, Wallace Thurman, Aaron Douglas, Claude McKay, Dorothy West, James Weldon Johnson, Nella Larsen, and the father of the blues, W. C. Handy.

While still at Lincoln, Hughes began collecting new poems for a second book that would be called *Fine Clothes to the Jew.*

Godmother Mason

Hughes shuttled back and forth between Lincoln and New York during his days at the university. One night in New York, he joined Van Vechten at Carnegie Hall for a concert of African-American spirituals. Although he didn't know it, it was going to be a very important night. In the audience was a wealthy widow named Charlotte van der Veer Quick Mason whose home was on Park Avenue. Like Van Vechten, Mason was a white person who loved black arts and culture. It didn't take long for Mason to grow very fond of Hughes. After their first meeting, she sent him away with a crisp fifty dollar bill. From that moment on, Hughes thought of Mason as his "godmother."

The summer of 1927 took Hughes to Tennessee and then Louisiana to experience the blues up close. While he was in New Orleans, Hughes suddenly had the urge to visit Havana, Cuba. Without thinking about it much, Hughes signed on as a common hand aboard the *Munloyal,* a small freighter heading to Havana from a New Orleans port. The trip to Havana was a short couple of weeks, but it brought back to Hughes memories of his days at sea on the *West Hassayampa* and *West Hesseltine.* Arriving safely back in New Orleans at the end of July, Hughes had only weeks remaining before the start of the school year at Lincoln. Quickly, he traveled from New Orleans to Biloxi, Mississippi, and then made his way to Mobile, Alabama. In Mobile he had quite a surprise. There, not far from the train station, Hughes spotted a familiar face. It was Zora Neale Hurston, the eccentric young writer he met years earlier in New York. She was returning to college in New York after spending the summer doing field work and conducting research in anthropology and folklore in Florida. Since both were traveling north, why not travel together? Hughes threw his bags into Hurston's car and together they set off for Pennsylvania and New York.

After a brief stop at Lincoln, Hughes was determined to visit Godmother Mason, who was as eager to reunite with Hughes as he was to reconnect with her. She listened, spellbound, to his adventures down South. When Hughes ended his report of his summer travels and of all the wonderful, exciting black people he met down there who were working, singing, and living a blues life, Godmother Mason was hit with a great idea. Hughes should write about what he had seen and heard. He should write a novel! Not the kind of woman one can say no to, Godmother Mason was sure it was the perfect project for Hughes to do. But Hughes did not want to write a novel. Although he had dabbled in musical theater and short-story writing and proved he was a versatile writer, writing a novel held no appeal for him. But he could not disappoint Godmother Mason. She had been very generous to Hughes. "She is so entirely wonderful," he told others (quoted in Rampersad, 1.154). Still, sitting down to write a novel was no easy task. It was September, the beginning of a new school year at Lincoln. Uninspired and busy with his classes, Hughes's novel writing went slowly. Very slowly indeed. To free him from the worries about money she believed were keeping him from making progress on his novel, Godmother Mason made Hughes an offer he could not refuse. She offered to send him $150 each month for a year if he would only attend school and write. It was an incredible sum of money at the time. It looked like life could get no better.

Hughes's agreement with Godmother Mason placed him, almost instantly, in the lap of luxury. He could now afford formal dinner attire. Godmother Mason shipped expensive writing paper to him at Lincoln. In a gleaming limousine, a white chauffeur drove him to the places he needed to go in New York. Hughes liked luxury. But his new life of ease made the drab living of Lincoln harder to bear. While having money meant fewer worries for Hughes, he made little progress on his novel in the first year of the agreement with Godmother Mason. Try as he might, he simply couldn't summon the inspiration required for a book his heart was not in. He fancied himself a poet, true enough, but hardly a novelist. With his novel at a standstill, a folk opera he was planning with Hurston only vaguely conceived, and a new play he was imagining on Toussaint

L'Ouverture and the Haitian Revolution going nowhere, Hughes was in an unusual rut. Although Godmother Mason had hoped for the opposite outcome, her doting "was lulling her boy into a sweet drowse" (Rampersad, 1. 161).

Time came and went with little to show for Godmother Mason's investment in Hughes. She began to question Hughes about his month-to-month spending, and he was impatient with her demand that he provide her a summary report of all his expenses to date. Hughes was already submitting meticulous reports of his monthly expenses to Mason. To require a full summary of those reports, reports he neither copied for himself nor remembered in detail, felt unreasonable and, ultimately, oppressive. His adoration of and gratitude to her were deep; however, he could not confront Godmother Mason honestly about how impossible she was becoming. But he didn't have to. She lashed out at him first. Godmother Mason accused Hughes of being dishonest and ungrateful. Hughes was astonished by Godmother Mason's charges.

Back in his room at Lincoln, he tried to sort out his feelings. He wrote her a heartfelt letter. Although her excessive expectations of him frustrated Hughes, he wondered if his failure to write faster and change "rapidly enough into what you would have me to be" (quoted in Rampersad, 1.169) had been more difficult for her. He offered to end their financial relationship. Even as he gave her the opportunity to give up financial responsibility for him, though, he prayed she wouldn't. She didn't. Hughes was forgiven.

At the end of the summer of 1929, having graduated from Lincoln, Hughes moved into a room in the home of an African-American couple in New Jersey. With money from Godmother Mason still coming to him each month, Hughes worked hard over the fall and winter months to perfect his novel. He wanted nothing more than to please Godmother Mason. Three days after Valentine's Day, it was done. After two drafts that did not show Hughes's

ZORA NEALE HURSTON WAS ONE OF HUGHES'S FIRST
WRITER FRIENDS, AND LATER AN ENEMY. THIS PHOTO WAS
TAKEN BY CARL VAN VECHTEN, A GOOD FRIEND OF BOTH
AND A SUPPORTER OF THEIR WRITING.

best talent, the finished version of *Not Without Laughter*
was as close to perfect as Hughes could make it. Although
he had not even wanted to write a novel at first, getting it
done had turned into a labor of love. Hughes loved writing,
and he loved Godmother Mason. He felt like a load was
lifted off him when *Not Without Laughter* was finally off
his desk and out in the world. Knopf sent the first copies out
to San Francisco, Melbourne, Bombay, Tokyo, London, and
Paris. Hughes was suddenly an internationally known writer.

Severed Ties and the End of the Harlem Renaissance

Back in New Jersey, Hughes had a new neighbor. Zora Neale Hurston had moved in just down the street. It was a good thing since the two had been planning to work together for some time on a staged folk comedy to be called *Mule Bone*. The play was based on a short story of Hurston's called "The Bone of Contention." The story's plot was uncomplicated. Two men from the country go on a hunt together. A turkey is shot, but they debate which of them killed it. They fight. One hunter clobbers the other over the head with the hock bone of a mule. Found guilty of assault and battery, the guilty hunter is exiled from town forever. Full of wisecracks, folk humor, and southern dialect, *Mule Bone*, in which two men fight over a woman rather than a turkey, was riotously funny. It was a great disappointment to Hughes, then, when Hurston quit writing and suddenly moved back to New York. Hurston promised to keep working on it but did not do so. Finishing the play seemed to be a lost cause.

Although giving up on *Mule Bone* disappointed Hughes deeply, he was about to be even more disappointed. Once again, Godmother Mason was unhappy with Hughes. She said he was not working fast enough and was taking too much time off. The pressure on Hughes was more than he could bear. He rebelled. They argued bitterly. In the end, Hughes asked Godmother Mason to release him from her support. This time he was serious. Hughes borrowed two hundred dollars from Van Vechten to get by. One of the longest and most important relationships of Hughes's career was over.

For many months afterward, Hughes was sad. He could not hide his gloom easily. With Hurston gone, and feeling rejected by Godmother Mason, Hughes had no one left to talk to. To keep busy, Hughes threw himself into theater. But nothing could keep his mind off Godmother Mason. His gloom turned to sickness. He needed a change of scenery. Early in 1931, telling no one, Hughes left New Jersey for Ohio. Much to his surprise, a local theater group there was preparing to mount the unfinished play, *Mule Bone*. They had gotten it from Van Vechten, who had gotten it from Hurston. Hughes was even more surprised to find out that Hurston claimed to be the play's only author. His name was nowhere on it. Secretly copyrighting it several months earlier, Hurston claimed to have composed *Mule Bone* entirely on her own. Hughes was astounded. He was unaware of ill feelings and petty jealousies, professional and romantic, that were at the bottom of this incredible shock.

From the beginning, the *Mule Bone* collaboration involved more than the two coauthors. Hughes brought to their collaboration the secretarial services of Louise Thompson, the estranged wife of the eccentric Wallace Thurman. Thompson had been hired a year earlier by Godmother Mason as an assistant to Hughes. For the *Mule Bone* project, Thompson was enlisted to type as Hurston and Hughes invented dialogue. The energy was high and, with Thompson's fast fingers, Hurston and Hughes made quick progress. But Thompson apparently had so much of Hughes's attention when the three of them were not working together that Hurston felt jilted. Growing moody and becoming more and more difficult to work with, Hurston abruptly abandoned the play and moved to Manhattan. While Hurston's promise to continue work on the play (it was close to completion) reassured Hughes somewhat, he assumed that her promise meant she would work on it *with* him. Hughes did not hear any more from Hurston concerning *Mule Bone*, however, until he threatened legal action over the rights to the play and its authorship. Although Hurston wrote to Godmother Mason, as she tried to explain her feud with Hughes, that she entertained no romantic interest in Hughes, all along, according to Hughes biographer Rampersad, Hurston "had acted like a lover spurned" (1.197).

Hurston's jealousy of Hughes's apparently nonexistent romance with Thompson—Hurston only imagined one where, according to Thompson, none existed—was only the most direct cause of Hughes's troubles in 1930. Hughes's relationship with Godmother Mason was strained. Hurston's melodramatic complaints to Mason about Hughes's "vile" behavior and their conflict over *Mule Bone* only deepened Mason's distrust of Hughes (quoted in Rampersad, 1.196). Long unhappy with the slow pace of Hughes's writing, Godmother Mason put Hughes totally out of her favor now. Hurston was only partly responsible for feeding Mason's increasing bitterness toward Hughes, though. Alain Locke, also under Godmother Mason's financial stewardship, contributed as much as Hurston to Hughes's final rejection by Mason, probably for similar reasons.

Locke, too, had been enamored of Hughes for some time—since their days in Paris, in fact. Once joining Locke on a trip from Paris to Italy almost ten years earlier in 1924, Hughes spent five pleasant days in Locke's company touring the Mediterranean town of Genoa at Locke's invitation. Whether or not a romantic tryst took place between them in Italy, it was Locke's hope that Hughes would share the attraction and that a relationship would ensue. Whatever the details of their travels together, it is certain that Hughes had no desire to enter into a sustained romantic relationship with Locke. His cold shoulder to Locke's romantic interest in him may not have been because Locke was a man, however.

Although it is widely believed by most biographers and critics of Hughes's works that Hughes was gay, it is an assumption even his closest friends could not verify, perhaps because Hughes was especially secretive about his love affairs. A few of his friends believed Hughes was neither heterosexual nor homosexual, but rather asexual, without having much interest in erotic relationships with men or women, even if he had a few romantic encounters with both. According to Hughes's biographer Laurie Leach, "whatever his sexual orientation, his characteristic response to those who displayed or returned erotic interest was evasion" (79). Perhaps Locke grew to resent Hughes's rejection as had Hurston. For it was Locke's self-interested, negative reports to Godmother Mason on the progress of the work Hughes had undertaken with Hurston that lit the fuse to Mason's angry and final parting with Hughes. Hughes had been betrayed as a result of occasionally taking Locke into his confidence. In mocking tones Locke would later exult in Hughes's ruined relationship with Mason. Although Locke was already in Mason's good graces and receiving a (comparatively modest) check from her somewhat regularly, Hughes's loss became Locke's financial gain.

Siding with Hurston in her battle with Hughes over *Mule Bone*, Mason broke with Hughes coldly and unsympathetically. When he hoped to reconcile with her, she did not even grant him an audience. Miserable about losing Godmother Mason and Locke, Hughes hoped to salvage his relationship with Hurston. With the threat of a lawsuit still pending, he offered her a deal. Both of them would share royalties from the play's production, but Hurston would get slightly more. Hughes cared little for the money. He needed friends desperately. Hurston agreed to the deal. The split was over. Or seemed over to Hughes.

Hurston's antics continued. Meeting Hughes in Cleveland to settle their agreement, Hurston discovered that Louise Thompson was in town, too. Thompson's presence in Cleveland was purely a coincidence, since, thanks to Hurston's own misrepresentation of Hughes's relationship with Thompson, Mason had terminated her. But Hurston would not be appeased. In a public fit of rage, she cruelly defamed Hughes. The prospect of saving his friendship with Hurston was dead. Symbolically, Hughes's associations with Mason, Locke, and Hurston that year ended at exactly the time the whole renaissance movement was coming to an equally abrupt end.

"That spring for me (and, I guess, all of us) was the end of the Harlem Renaissance," Hughes would write in his autobiography. "We were no longer in vogue, anyway, we Negroes" (*The Big Sea*, 334). Some African-American artists were going hungry, and, with the stock market crash of 1929, the money of generous patrons had all but dried up. Still, Hughes was dedicated to making a living at writing. Checks from Godmother Mason were no longer coming to him, but the Harmon Gold Award for Literature and four hundred dollars in prize money was his inspiration. It was the biggest sum of money Hughes ever had in hand at one time. It was enough to finance a three-month visit to Cuba and Haiti. Although he would get the chance to meet some of the most important poets of these two island nations (Nicolás Guillén in Cuba and Jacques Roumain in Haiti), this trip was not as important as the ones soon to come to places at greater distances than these.

Russia and Spain

With the Great Depression, the Harlem Renaissance came to a screeching halt. Far fewer patrons were supporting far fewer artists, black or white. Some of the wealthiest Americans lost their fortunes. The Roaring Twenties were over, throwing into question, for many, the grand romance with capitalism that was supposed to sustain the prosperity that the stock market crash of 1929 brought to such a catastrophic end. Many Americans, suffering miserably and disillusioned by capitalism, looked to other economic and social systems as an alternative to America's capitalist failure. In Soviet Communism, Hughes, and a number of other black artists, many political radicals, believed they saw the shimmering glimpses of a society free from economic exploitation and, importantly, racism. With a group of twenty-one Americans recruited by Louise Thompson, Hughes set sail on board the *Europa* on June 14, 1932, for Russia.

The group had been invited to Moscow by local officials to help make a film on American race relations. Several writers, actors, and singers were part of the group. Most of them held radical views about the problem of racism in the United States, but their views on communism, the form of government in the Soviet Union, varied widely. A few only imagined the trip as a leisurely way of passing the summer.

Hughes admired Moscow immensely. Not only were its buildings stately and its landscape picturesque, racism seemed completely absent from the city. In fact, a large statue of the national poet, Alexander Pushkin, standing in the city's central square, seemed like a sign of the Soviets' color blindness. Pushkin, the great Russian, was a black man. Although Hughes and his companions were mostly unknown to the people of Moscow, they were treated like stars. Despite their popularity, Hughes was disappointed that progress on the film project he was there to work on was slow and full of hurdles. A bad script, language barriers, and repeated delays nearly cancelled the whole project. In the end the problems facing the filmmakers were so big that the film, *Black and White*, had to be postponed. Soon it was clear that it could not be made before the group of twenty-two Americans returned to the United States. For Hughes and his friends, the film project was a disaster.

As payment for the group's time and expenses, the Soviets offered all twenty-two the chance to tour the Soviet Union. A few members of the group dismissed the idea and left immediately for the United States. Some who didn't have any immediate obligations stayed. Hughes was one of them. Despite the troubles with *Black and White*, Hughes felt a freedom in Russia that he did not feel anywhere in the

AFTER HIS TRIP TO THE SOVIET UNION, HUGHES TRAVELED
ALL OVER CENTRAL ASIA WITH A TYPEWRITER, A VICTROLA,
AND HIS CURIOSITY.

United States. He became more convinced of communism's strengths, particularly its call to the workers of the world to unite in a revolution against capitalism's control of the world's wealth. Once the future of *Black and White* had been settled, Hughes could enjoy Russia's freedoms without the worry of a failing film project and the disgruntled black Americans who had sacrificed to see it through. He put his new beliefs into a new poem called "Good Morning, Revolution":

> Good-morning, Revolution:
> You're the very best friend
> I ever had.
> We gonna pal around together from now on.
> (*Collected Poems*, 162)

The freedoms he enjoyed in the Soviet Union as a black man made leaving difficult, although his friends in New York begged Hughes to return home. Hughes traveled all over the Soviet Union and Central Asia with a typewriter, a victrola, and a collection of recordings by jazz and blues greats Louis Armstrong and Ethel Waters. After nearly a year and a half, Hughes returned to the United States. The international tour had been thrilling, but his life, and his people, were in the United States. When Hughes landed stateside, he did not return to New York. Instead, he went to California. There, friends met him in San Francisco, and one of them offered Hughes the use of his cottage at Carmel-By-the-Sea, a historic artist's colony midway between San Francisco and Los Angeles. Hughes planned to spend a year in the cottage earning his living by writing. Already he had finished the beginning of a book of short stories in Asia. To complete that project and earn his living at writing, Hughes wrote ten to twelve hours each day for months. When they were finally finished, many of those stories were collected in Hughes's first book of short stories, *The Ways of White Folks*.

In the summer of 1937, Hughes left the country again. This time he headed for Spain. In order to earn his keep in Spain, Hughes agreed to work as a foreign correspondent for the *Baltimore Afro-American*, the *Cleveland Call and Post*, and *Globe* magazine. Although it was another meaningful trip for Hughes, Spain was a much less thrilling experience than Russia. A Spanish civil war had been declared and the sound of nighttime air raids made Hughes perpetually uneasy. However, among the suffering Spanish, Hughes noted the many black North Africans (Moors) and dark-skinned Cubans who had come to Spain, some part of the Spanish military, as well as more than a few black Americans living or fighting in Spain. "I met all kinds of Negroes in Spain, just as I'd met all kinds in Harlem," he recalled later. This melting pot of black people from across the globe was a special curiosity of Hughes's, since they appeared to come and go in Spanish society without anyone seeming to notice their much darker color, or to care. "All the Negroes, of whatever nationality, to whom I talked," Hughes wrote "agreed that there was not the slightest color prejudice in Spain" (*I Wonder*, 351). As both Spain and the Soviet Union seemed to show, seeing the wider world was an opportunity for Hughes, so familiar with American racism, to experience the possibility of life without racial prejudice. As dangerous as living in Spain was in 1937, it had its appeal.

With the war in Spain worsening, and food getting more and more scarce, Hughes finally packed his belongings— books, a typewriter, some souvenirs, a bottle of wine from a friend—and left, sorrowfully, months later. Hughes had fallen in love with Spain in spite of its perils, and, having learned some Spanish along the way, he wondered if he would ever see it again. He wondered what would become of the Spanish people. The crisis in Spain brought thoughts of people, like the Spanish, "walking the tightropes everywhere—the tightrope of color in Alabama, the tight- rope of transition in the Soviet Union, the tightrope of repression in Japan, the tightrope of fear of war in France— and of war itself in China and in Spain . . . Anybody is liable to fall off a tightrope in any land," Hughes concluded on taking leave of Spain, "and God help you if you fall the wrong way" (*I Wonder*, 400).

World War II

By the early 1940s a very fervent sense of patriotism was overtaking America. World War II was under way in Europe and, with the December bombing of Pearl Harbor, America was soon to enter the fray. A strong pro-American feeling was in the air. American values, including Christianity and faith in the good of government, were unshakeable. Hughes was made from another cast, however. He had spent the majority of the 1930s developing an equally passionate, but opposite, radical philosophy. Like many black artists after the Harlem Renaissance, Hughes had lost faith in his home country. His own experiences with racial hatred and segregation, the stock market crash of 1929, and the Great Depression that followed caused him to question just how democratic America really was. At the same time that American patriotism began to grow, then, there was already a deep suspicion about America's vaunted values. Before long, America would demonstrate a deeper distrust of Hughes.

Hughes's faith in American democracy and racial equality did not decline all at once. Rather, over the next twenty-five years until his death, his faith in America ebbed and flowed. Late in 1941, for instance, Hughes was hopeful again, seeing the American attack on fascism abroad as a promising prelude to the overthrow of the customs of Jim Crow at home.That hopefulness Hughes reflected in "Jim Crow's Last Stand," a poem inspired by the heroic actions of an African-American messman named "Dorie" Miller who, under Japanese attack at Pearl Harbor, took control of a machine gun on board the besieged

USS *West Virginia* and, it is alleged, shot down as many as six enemy aircrafts. He was awarded the Navy Cross for his heroics:

> Pearl Harbor put Jim Crow on the run.
> That Crow can't fight for Democracy
> And be the same old Crow he used to be—
> Although right now, even yet today,
> He still tries to act in the same old way.
> But India and China and Harlem, too,
> Have made up their minds Jim Crow is through.
>
> When Dorie Miller took gun in hand—
> Jim Crow started his last stand.
> Our battle yet is far from won
> But when it is, Jim Crow'll be done.
> We gonna bury that son-of-a-gun!
> (*Collected Poems*, 299)

Despite his optimism, Hughes was not unaware of how "far" the country was from winning the "battle" against Jim Crow. Although President Roosevelt had signed Executive Order 8802 six months earlier, forbidding discrimination in the defense industry, discrimination in the armed forces continued to vex U.S. race relations, especially in the South. In the navy, African Americans were permitted only to serve in non-combat roles. The Red Cross kept the blood of black soldiers and white soldiers apart so that no white soldiers risked receiving "black" blood. Still, Roosevelt's Executive Order 8802 and the obvious heroism of African-American servicemen and servicewomen in the face of on-going discrimination were signs enough to Hughes that Jim Crow would fall by the same weapons that would defeat fascism overseas.

Hughes did not hope idly for the end of Jim Crow, however. Late in October 1942, facing the war draft, he responded to a questionnaire from the Selective Service angrily protesting segregation in the armed forces. Later, in a regular column for the *Chicago Defender* newspaper and in a pamphlet of poems inspired by the interlocking ideals of patriotism and race pride found in "Jim Crow's Last Stand," Hughes issued a clear condemnation of the injustices that kept African Americans from feeling included in the principles of "liberty and justice for all." Early the next year, men over the age of thirty-eight were released from the draft rolls. At forty-one, Hughes avoided being called up for service, but he remained a vocal critic of the armed services and their policies of racial prejudice.

It was also 1943 when Hughes introduced his most famous persona, Jesse B. Simple, in his *Chicago Defender* column "Here to Yonder." The column featured colorful conversations between Hughes's comical "Simple Minded Friend" and a grave narrator. A Southerner recently come North, Jesse B. Simple, or Semple, was something like Hughes's alter ego. Where Hughes was a serious critic of the war, politics, and race relations, Simple approached these topics with rare wit, sometimes hilarity. A womanizer with a disgruntled wife and two women on the side—one prim and proper, the other loud and garish—Simple is part country boy, part Harlem hipster. His politics are misinformed but commonsensical and full of straight-faced humor.

For twenty-three years Hughes endeared Simple to a national audience. So popular was Simple with the readers of the *Chicago Defender* that, beginning in 1950, Hughes collected his columns into a series of five books. In Jesse B. Simple Hughes created one of the twentieth century's most beloved satirical characters and wrote himself into a long line of American humorists. Jesse B. Simple secured Hughes's popular appeal for years and years to come.

Facing McCarthy

The fact that Hughes had achieved international fame did not keep his vision of his role in the world from being local. He remained committed to reaching people on the ground with his art. More and more, he wanted to reach younger generations as well. So in the fall of 1944, with the help of the Common Council for American Unity and *Common Ground* magazine, he planned to tour the country, visiting high schools, reading his work, and addressing their students. At black high schools he aimed to instill in students a sense of race pride. At white high schools he set out to demonstrate African-American intelligence and creativity. It was an admirable plan. Before it could get under way, however, Hughes was called up by the U.S. House of Representatives Special Committee on Un-American Activities to defend himself against charges that he was a Communist Party member intent upon overthrowing the U.S. government. Almost immediately, high schools where Hughes planned to read canceled his visits.

Hughes strongly denied the charges, many of them false rumors attributed to the bad intelligence of the Federal Bureau of Investigations (FBI). On the strength of his defense and the reputation of the Common Council for American Unity, though, some of the canceled visits were reinstated. Eventually, Hughes made his way to Philadelphia and several large and small cities in New Jersey and upstate New York. Although the tour was physically taxing on Hughes, the Common Council, school administrators, and students alike considered it a triumph. The next year the FBI removed his name from their list of prominent Communists. Unfortunately, it was not the end of Hughes's troubles with the government and its Communist obsession.

Hughes tried to leave behind the resentment he felt for all of the problems he faced because of the false reports of Communist Party membership during two teaching appointments at

On March 27, 1953, Langston Hughes was called to testify before a Senate subcommittee because of Joseph McCarthy's witch hunt against American leftists.

Atlanta University in 1949 and the University of Chicago's Laboratory School in 1948. A visiting professor of creative writing at Atlanta and a visiting lecturer at Chicago, Hughes taught poetry to Atlanta undergraduates and Chicago youth. Because teaching did not require him to travel so frequently, the two semesters he stood before wide-eyed students in Atlanta and Chicago protected him from the angry complaints of paranoid Americans whose distortions of the poet's character routinely threatened his ability to make a living.

The relief was temporary, though. Neither full-time teaching nor his success at finding a notable conductor to stage a production of his opera, *Troubled Island*, could prevent the Senate Permanent Subcommittee on Investigations, infamously led by Senator Joseph McCarthy, from issuing Hughes a subpoena five years later, just when it looked as though the allegations concerning his Communist affiliation had been put to rest. It was March 1953. Senator McCarthy and his allies were on a witch hunt for Communist subversives and sympathizers. Yet again, Hughes was being called upon to answer for his art. McCarthy and his committee had deemed approximately sixteen of Hughes's twenty-five or so published books plausibly dangerous.

Hughes appeared before McCarthy's committee poised and well practiced for the event. He succeeded in resisting the traps the committee's questions tried to lead him toward. If they could not get him to confess his own Communist convictions, then perhaps he would implicate others. Hughes was not so easily led. He implicated no one. Instead he trumpeted free speech, free press, and other civil liberties. He was neither a friendly witness nor a hostile one. It was a brilliant and most effective strategy. Longtime supporters praised him afterward. With the attacks on his character all but ended by the testimony before McCarthy and the Senate Permanent Subcommittee on Investigation, Hughes must have felt victorious in its aftermath. The government, at any rate, seemed ready to get past it. In the years to come, it would show Hughes a far friendlier face.

The Civil Rights Movement

Although his Senate hearing was behind him, Hughes was not so quick to let America forget its wrongs. Some of its worst offenses were still ongoing. Even though the federal government was making strides to dismantle racial segregation, the South continued to be stubbornly set against racial integration. By the early 1950s the stubbornness of the southern states to permit African Americans to vote without being harassed, or to integrate public schools, transportation, hotels, parks, and restaurants, was at fever pitch. The Civil Rights, or Freedom, Movement—the dangerous struggle of African Americans to confront the racist power structure of the South and to insist upon "liberty and justice for all"—was picking up steam in response. Organizing marches, rallies, sit-ins, and other demonstrations, civil rights activists like the Reverend Dr. Martin Luther King Jr. and the Student Nonviolent Coordinating Committee (SNCC) put their lives on the line to protest the South's injustices toward its African-American citizens. Although Hughes was a strong advocate of the principles of the Civil Rights Movement, oddly, he was not a very visible part of the struggle. Despite his wide recognition, even fame in some circles, "he participated in relatively few demonstrations, read about the March on Washington in a Paris newspaper instead of joining the crowd on the mall, declined an invitation to join Dr. Martin Luther King in Alabama, and, as he cut back on lecturing in the final years of his life, rarely spoke publicly on the issue" (Leach, 139).

Naturally, some doubted Hughes's commitment to the Civil Rights Movement, but Hughes remained true to African-American freedom and equality. Where others protested with their bodies, Hughes continued to protest with his pen. In the *Chicago Defender*, for example, he criticized the great Mississippi novelist William Faulkner, winner of a Nobel Prize, for expressing the opinion that integration in Mississippi should go much more slowly than civil rights protesters and the federal government desired. Faulkner insisted on a more moderate and patient pace for social change, but Hughes and many others insisted that African Americans had been moderate and patient long enough and that the time for justice was now, not some distant time in the future.

LANGSTON HUGHES WAS POPULAR THROUGHOUT HIS LIFE. HERE, HE SIGNS AUTOGRAPHS FOR THE CHILDREN WHO SURROUND HIM.

Go *slow*, they say—
While the bite
Of the dog is fast.
Go *slow*, I hear—
While they tell me
You can't eat here!
You can't live here!
You can't work here!
Don't demonstrate! Wait!—
While they lock the gate. (*Collected Poems*, 537)

But with the movement intensifying, many expected more than just a poem like "Go Slow" or newspaper columns from Hughes. His protest of Faulkner was but a small contribution to a movement that was growing far more serious than a squabble between a black and white writer. Just as the Civil Rights Movement was reaching its most critical point in the early 1960s, and growing violent as a result, it seemed that Hughes was moving further and further away from the struggle.

Ultimately Hughes went to work on a new play, *Jericho-Jim Crow*, which redeemed Hughes in the eyes of his critics who had come to believe that Hughes was washed up as a poet and no longer a significant literary figure to his people. *Jericho-Jim Crow* was satisfying to critics and civil rights figures alike. It ran for several months on Broadway and briefly revived Hughes's waning reputation. Unfortunately, because a newer, radical generation of proud African-American freedom fighters had taken over the civil rights scene, Hughes, despite *Jericho-Jim Crow*, did not fully recover his earlier glory as the premier poet of his people. In this period of black pride and black militancy, Hughes wrote little about his sense of his own blackness. Sadly, he was becoming outdated.

To portray Hughes as being pushed off the scene of black artistic life in the last ten years of his life would be incorrect, though. While other younger artists came to national prominence calling for a new black consciousness and a new black art that hearkened back to Africa, Hughes did not retire from his work. Nor was the importance of a lifetime of his art forgotten. In 1958, *Life* magazine called him "one of the blacks who brought honor to the United States" (Rampersad, 2.285). Very happily, just two years later he was awarded the prestigious Spingarn Medal, a major award issued by the NAACP for high and distinguished achievement by an African American.

If during the last years of his life Hughes was somewhat out of fashion with African Americans at home, especially the younger ones, past works of his were nevertheless reaching wider audiences abroad. Translations of popular works appeared in unlikely languages like Hindi, Czech, Arabic, and Japanese. Taking a renewed interest of his own in Africa, he published a collection entitled *An African Treasury: Articles, Essays, Stories, and Poems by Black*

Africans in 1960. It had been a well-received collection, leaving its reviewers unanimously "admiring it as a timely corrective to the traditional American ignorance of Africa" (Rampersad, 2.320). No doubt even Africans noticed this work. For at the end of the year, after forty years, Hughes made a return visit to Africa. He had been invited to Nigeria by Commander-in-Chief Benjamin Nnamdi Azikiwe, a former schoolmate from Lincoln. The visit so thrilled Hughes that he returned to Nigeria the very next year as a delegate to the American Society of African Culture. A month in Nigeria did not fully satisfy his renewed passion for all things African. Six months later he returned for yet another visit before going on to appointments and speaking engagements in Uganda and Ghana. He did not return home before visiting Egypt and Rome, Italy.

Back home his international appeal drew many foreign dignitaries. One of them, the Senegalese president Léopold Sédar Senghor, who was also a poet, issued a toast to Hughes at a White House dinner in 1961, announcing that Hughes had been an important influence on his own poetic works. Later, in 1962, Hughes was back in Washington, this time reading from his works at the first national poetry festival in American history. The response to him was tremendous; his lively reading earned him a resounding ovation. Perhaps the public enthusiasm also owed something also to his election the previous year into the National Institute of Arts and Letters.

Last Days

With all that was happening in the United States, 1965 took Hughes on a tour throughout Europe. Improbably, after so much trouble caused to him by the U.S. government under McCarthy's influence, Hughes went to Europe as a representative of the State Department. It was the last tour of his life. Two years later, on May 22, 1967, Hughes died at New York Polyclinic Hospital from complications following a surgery to remove an enlarged prostate. His funeral on May 25 was almost entirely a jazz concert with a few words and poems shared by Hughes's close friend, Arna Bontemps. It was what Hughes had requested. After the jazz pianist Randy Weston played a blues song he had written especially for Hughes, the funeral ended with one of Hughes's favorite jazz tunes, "Do Nothing Till You Hear from Me." Later, a small group of his closest friends gathered at the Ferncliff Crematory in Hartsdale, New York, to say their last goodbyes. Bowing their heads and reciting lines from "The Negro Speaks of Rivers," they wept while they witnessed his body's cremation and felt his soul leave them for a place "ancient as the world and older than the flow of human blood in human veins."

World War II brought African Americans in large numbers to the northern states, where blacks looked for opportunities unavailable in the Jim Crow South.

Chapter 2

The Harlem Renaissance

The literary achievements of Langston Hughes did not occur apart from a wider cultural movement. His work did, however, capture the spirit of that movement in African-American life like few others. While white America was celebrating the jazz age and the Roaring Twenties, black America was celebrating its own jazz and blues age. The flowering of black literature and poetry, of black music and dance, visual arts and pan-African politics in this era soon came to be identified as the Harlem Renaissance. Although its beginnings were as early as 1919, most accounts of the Harlem Renaissance agree that its most colorful years were between 1924 and the great stock market crash of 1929. Hughes was considered one of the leading voices of this movement, which found its most vibrant and diverse activity in and around the historic black enclave of Harlem in New York City. Hughes's 1926 essay, "The Negro Artist and the Racial Mountain," in fact, conveyed the meaning of the Harlem Renaissance as directly as any work before it.

Although his essay did not name the movement the "Harlem Renaissance," it was a manifesto for the new generation of black artists whose literary, musical, and artistic work defined the movement by departing from the unspoken but understood expectations of black writing that had come before. In contrast to the belief that black writers should only work to dignify the race by portraying only the most positive and polished images of black American life, Hughes countered in his essay:

> We younger Negro artists who create now intend to express our individual dark-skinned selves without fear or shame. If white people are pleased we are glad. If they are not, it doesn't matter. We know we are beautiful. And ugly too.
> ("The Negro Artist and the Racial Mountain," 95)

Hughes's position reflected a change in mood in black America, a mood brought on by the peculiar historical and cultural background that helped create it. Illuminating this background will help us better comprehend the courage, creativity, and genius of the most widely recognized black poet of the twentieth century.

World War I and the Returning Black Soldier

The mood in black America that eventually inspired the activity of the Harlem Renaissance was almost certainly affected by the expectations of black soldiers returning stateside from their fighting abroad. After risking their lives (and, for thousands, losing theirs) black men and women recognized the vast disparity between the great democratic principles their country called upon them to defend at war, and the stark racist reality of black life in America. After serving as "Soldiers of Democracy" overseas, as W. E. B. DuBois called them defiantly (5), black men and women came home to racial harassment, lynchings, voter intimidation, employment discrimination, and other designs to keep African Americans "in their places." But a new courage, even a new militancy, was evolving. America "is *our* fatherland," they cried. "It was right for us to fight" for it, and, although its shameful racist acts go on, "we would fight again. But by the God of Heaven, we are cowards and jackasses if now that that war is over, we do not marshal every ounce of our brain and brawn to fight a sterner, longer, more unbending battle against the forces of hell in our own land," proclaimed DuBois, (5). Although the historian David Levering Lewis has said that the mass movement of black radicalism led by Marcus Garvey was simultaneous with, but separate from, the new literary and arts movement, the hundreds of thousands of people of African descent nationwide who followed Garvey and his back-to-Africa philosophy shared the Harlem Renaissance's militant energy. It is no accident that Garvey frequently decked himself out in decorated military regalia. In a way, he embodied the militant mood taking hold of black Americans immediately after World War I. African Americans were asserting their civil rights and demanding social equality as they had never done before. In addition, the mass migration of blacks from the American South to the urban North also powerfully influenced the genesis of the Harlem Renaissance.

Harlem and the New Negro
When World War I closed the doors of European immigration to the United States that had been ongoing since the 1880s, northern industry required new labor pools. A boll weevil infestation, which destroyed cotton plants in the South, and an epidemic of lynchings there provoked a new wave of black migration north. During the war years, an estimated 30,000 African Americans found work on the railroads, about 27,000 in shipbuilding, and an additional 75,000 in coal mining. By 1918 an estimated one million African Americans had already left the South and millions more would follow (Kent, 30–31).

Not only did the Great Black Migration from the rural south to the industrial north concentrate black people into new dynamic living arrangements, but the migration of African Americans was accompanied by an equally significant influx of people from the West Indies to America's urban centers. The new black imigrants to the north were hardly welcome, however.

The end of World War I brought spectacular violence to black people living in the north as white Americans acted out their fears of having to compete with blacks for jobs during peacetime. In 1919 alone, for example, race riots broke out in approximately twenty-five U.S. cities, seventy blacks were lynched, and fourteen were publicly burned—eleven of them while alive. Perhaps only in Harlem, New York, did African Americans and West Indians arrive at their new northern homes without significant violence. There, "thousands of Negroes pour[ed] into Harlem month by month," reported the poet James Weldon Johnson in his 1930 historical account of African Americans in New York City, *Black Manhattan*. "Although there was bitter feeling in Harlem during the fifteen years of struggle the Negro went through in getting a foothold on the land," he wrote, "there was never any demonstration of violence that could be called serious" (35).

Devoid of the racist violence of other major cities, it was not long before uptown New York City was transformed into the most famous enclave of black life in American history. Harlem was the perfect place for a black arts and cultural renaissance to occur, not least because the "time and the circumstances of its creation made Harlem symbolize the Afro-American's coming of age" (Huggins, *Harlem*, 13). While other U.S. cities had their own "darktowns," districts inside the city limits made up of black transplants from the South, Harlem was the center of a dramatic transformation in the character of African-American social and political thought. The "New Negro" called Harlem his home.

Determined to accept his second-class citizenship in America no longer, the New Negro would refuse to "turn the other cheek" after the war. He rejected the stereotypes about him and insisted on racial respect and social equality.

HARLEM WAS THE CENTER OF THE ARTS FOR AFRICAN AMERICANS IN THE POST-WAR YEARS. HERE IT IS DEPICTED BY JACOB LAWRENCE, A PREMIER PAINTER IN THE HARLEM RENAISSANCE YEARS AND BEYOND.

This new assertiveness, even militancy, was given poetic voice by the Jamaican-born poet Claude McKay in his verse "If We Must Die."

> If we must die, let it not be like hogs
> Hunted and penned in an inglorious spot,
> While round us bark the mad and hungry dogs,
> Making their mock at our accursed lot.
> If we must die, O let us nobly die,
> So that our precious blood may not be shed
> In vain; then even the monsters we defy
> Shall be constrained to honor us though dead!
> O kinsmen we must meet the common foe!
> Though far outnumbered let us show us brave,
> And for their thousand blows deal one deathblow!
> What though before us lies the open grave?
> Like men we'll face the murderous, cowardly pack,
> Pressed to the wall, dying, but fighting back! (1007)

Thus emboldened, the New Negro had specific social and political goals to reach as well: higher wages, fewer working hours, increased job opportunities, greater economic security, and bargaining power. In short the New Negro wanted justice and would not settle for less. The New Negro showed a new confidence born of the bravery of military service. When New York's Fifteenth Infantry Regiment, a regiment of African-American volunteers, came proudly home, marching in lockstep up Lenox Avenue to 145th Street, they brought an uncompromising dignity to Harlem and stirred proud racial feelings within it. As historian Nathan Huggins writes,

> the Fifteenth Infantry Regiment marched down Fifth Avenue in massive company phalanxes. Black American, fighting men. Lieutenant James Europe's band, which had made itself and the new American jazz famous throughout France, led them down the broad avenue under flags and banners reading: OUR HEROES—WELCOME HOME. Through throngs of cheering New Yorkers, they marched, through the newly erected victory arch at 25th Street, past the public library, continuing up Fifth Avenue to 110th Street and the end of Central Park. Then it was over to Lenox Avenue and up that street, through Harlem to 145th Street. On these uptown streets, they changed their tight phalanxes to an open formation. The cheering crowds were darker with familiar accents; they called out names and ran within the ranks to touch the men. Jim Europe's band of sixty brass and reed, thirty trumpet swung into "Here Comes My Daddy Now"; all Harlem went wild. (*Harlem*, 55–56)

The Fifteenth Infantry's victory parade energized Harlem and announced a new era of cultural vitality and racial assertiveness.

The new black assertiveness found its most prolific spokesman in the distinguished scholar and race leader W. E. B. DuBois. The Harvard-trained intellectual had set the tone for the New Negro movement as early as 1903 with his collection of essays, *The Souls of Black Folk*. In that work DuBois criticized the historical habit of African-American patience and long-suffering. He departed from the faith other black leaders had in the goodwill of whites to achieve racial equality. Instead, he insisted on the immediate recognition of the political rights of all Americans and upon black self-determination, not white wealth or goodwill.

Soon, DuBois and the newly formed NAACP were identified with the new black pride and racial boldness. Establishing themselves in Harlem shortly before the war, DuBois and the NAACP were a particularly powerful draw for young African-American artists and intellectuals. "Without perhaps knowing it," DuBois and the NAACP "were attracting young Negroes to New York because they symbolized the new spirit that the postwar generation felt" (Huggins, *Harlem*, 21).

As the editor in chief of the *Crisis*, the monthly publication of the association, DuBois helped cultivate the talents of the young artists and writers that the new mood in Harlem drew there. Many of the most widely recognized poets, playwrights, and would-be novelists associated with the Harlem Renaissance had their first national publications in the pages of the *Crisis*. In June 1921, Langston Hughes's first published poem, "The Negro Speaks of Rivers," appeared there.

Besides the important space afforded to new black writers in the *Crisis*, two other magazines helped feed the fire of arts and literature inspiring the Harlem Renaissance. Hoping to compete with the *Crisis* for New Negro readers, the *Messenger* claimed to be "The Only Radical Negro Magazine in America." In 1923 the NAACP's sister organization, the Urban League, began publishing its own literary organ, *Opportunity*. As important as

IN 1921, LANGSTON HUGHES'S FIRST PUBLISHED POEM APPEARED IN THE *CRISIS*, THE MONTHLY PUBLICATION OF THE NAACP.

all three magazines were to the early careers of the most famous Harlem Renaissance writers, they provided the formal launching pad for the national reach of the Harlem Renaissance and set its literary course. But it was Charles Johnson, the new editor of *Opportunity*, who first succeeded in bringing these writers together under one festive roof.

In March 1924 Johnson hosted a celebration of Negro writing at Manhattan's Civic Club, an exclusive New York supper club that did not discriminate on the basis of race or gender. He invited about a dozen emerging poets and writers to the gathering, which would also include several established writers. On this occasion famous white writers, including playwright Eugene O'Neill and satirist H. L. Mencken, would show up to socialize with new black talents not yet widely known: Eric Walrond, Jessie Fauset, Countee Cullen, Gwendolyn Bennet, and Georgia Douglass Johnson. (Hughes, unfortunately, was away in Europe.) DuBois and James Weldon Johnson were also present, as was a young Howard University philosophy professor, Alain Locke, the first African-American Rhodes Scholar, who served as the evening's master of ceremonies.

This Civic Club event solidified the movement and inspired Locke, who would become known as the dean of the Harlem Renaissance, to his most important contribution to African-American literature: a collection of poems, art, dramatic pieces, and essays by various up-and-coming writers (many of whom attended the Civic Club gathering) he titled *The New Negro*.

Locke's *The New Negro* (1925) did in print what Johnson's Civic Club dinner did in person. It gathered the most important new black writers and artists in a single volume, implicitly announcing a New Negro movement in full swing. Locke's own essay, "The New Negro," opened the collection. In it he heralded a "new phase of group development," a "spiritual Coming of Age" for black Americans (16). The new feeling of the African American had yielded two new sensibilities. The first looked on the black folk culture anew. It no longer repudiated it as uncivilized, crude, and unsuited to racial respect. Rather, it recognized the "very substantial contributions" (15) of the black folk class to American folk art, especially music. Coming out of this tradition, jazz, spirituals, and the blues significantly influenced the artistic output of the Harlem Renaissance, not least Hughes's own poetry.

According to Locke's pioneering essay, the other new sensibility growing out of the "new spirit" in Harlem was one recognizing Africa and its descendents worldwide as having common interests and a common destiny. "As with the Jew, persecution is making the Negro international," Locke wrote (14). Africa was the homeland, and the new African-American internationalism made colonialism

OPPORTUNITY COMPETED WITH THE *CRISIS* AS THE VOICE OF THE AFRICAN-AMERICAN ART WORLD. LANGSTON HUGHES PUBLISHED WORK IN BOTH MAGAZINES.

and African development just as urgent to the New Negro in Harlem as social equality and economic development at home. In this sense, too, the New Negro was nothing if not modern. His home was in Harlem but his mind reached well past Harlem toward places oceans away.

Today, the Harlem Renaissance is seen in two phases. The first, called the period of primary black propaganda, extended from 1921 to 1924. Charles Johnson's Civic Club affair was the capstone event of the period. It represented the New Negro's coming-out party, as all that the New Negro stood for was, by then, plain to see. The second phase of the Harlem Renaissance was characterized by the added impetus of white patronage. Between 1924 and 1931 a significant number of the young writers and artists associated with the Harlem Renaissance movement found financial backing with wealthy white patrons who took a keen interest in what was happening in Harlem. It was a period, as Hughes called it in his autobiography, *The Big Sea*, "when the Negro was in vogue" with black *and* white Americans. The financial generosity of a few wealthy white patrons was as important to the cultivation of new black talent as the black editors and civil rights figures who published and promoted them. For as long as there was significant white wealth in New York to underwrite its literary and artistic activity, the Harlem Renaissance endured.

With the 1929 stock market crash and the Depression coming on its heels, however, the artistic and cultural outpouring that had been the Harlem Renaissance came slowly to a halt. By 1931 the movement had run its course, but not before Hughes had become its most celebrated artist. As with few other artists of his day, the Harlem Renaissance came to be nearly defined by Hughes's poems and plays. "No Negro writer so completely symbolizes the new emancipation of the Negro mind," Charles Johnson proclaimed in 1925 (210). No African-American writer gave the Harlem Renaissance so restless, colorful, and vigorous a voice as Hughes.

Got the Weary Blues And can't be satisfied— I ain't happy no mo' And I wish that I had died." "I got the Weary Blue And I can't be satisfied. Got the Weary Blues And can't be satisfied— I ain't happy no mo' And I wish that I had died." "I got the Weary Blue And I can't be satisfied. Got the Weary Blues And can't be satisfied— I ain't happy no mo' And I wish that I had died." "I got the Weary Blue And I can't be satisfied. Got the Weary Blues And can't be satisfied— I ain't happy no mo' And I wish that I had died." "I got the Weary Blue And I can't be satisfied. Got the Weary Blues And can't be satisfied— I ain't happy no mo' And I wish that I had died." "I got the Weary Blue And I can't be satisfied. Got the Weary Blues And can't be satisfied— I ain't happy no mo' And I wish that I had died." "I got the Weary Blue And I can't be satisfied. Got the Weary Blues And can't be satisfied— I ain't happy no mo' And I wish that I had died." "I got the Weary Blue And I can't be satisfied. Got the Weary Blues And can't be satisfied— I ain't happy no mo' And I wish that I had died." "I got the Weary Blue And I can't be satisfied. Got the Weary

Part II:
The Major Works

lues And can't be satisfied— I ain't happy no mo' And I
hat I had died.""I got the Weary Blue And I can't be sati
ot the Weary Blues And can't be satisfied— I ain't happy
nd I wish that I had died.""I got the Weary Blue And I
e satisfied. Got the Weary Blues And can't be satisfi
in't happy no mo' And I wish that I had died.""I got the
lue And I can't be satisfied. Got the Weary Blues And ca
atisfied— I ain't happy no mo' And I wish that I had di
ot the Weary Blue And I can't be satisfied. Got the Weary
nd can't be satisfied— I ain't happy no mo' And I wish t
ad died.""I got the Weary Blue And I can't be satisfie
ne Weary Blues And can't be satisfied— I ain't happy
nd I wish that I had died.""I got the Weary Blue And I
e satisfied. Got the Weary Blues And can't be satisfi
in't happy no mo' And I wish that I had died.""I got the
lue And I can't be satisfied. Got the Weary Blues And ca
atisfied— I ain't happy no mo' And I wish that I had di
ot the Weary Blue And I can't be satisfied. Got the Weary
nd can't be satisfied— I ain't happy no mo' And I wish t
ad died.""I got the Weary Blue And I can't be satisfie
ne Weary Blues And can't be satisfied— I ain't happy
nd I wish that I had died.""I got the Weary Blue And I
e satisfied. Got the Weary Blues And can't be satisfi
in't happy no mo' And I wish that I had died.""I got the
lue And I can't be satisfied. Got the Weary Blues And ca
atisfied— I ain't happy no mo' And I wish that I had di
ot the Weary Blue And I can't be satisfied. Got the Weary
nd can't be satisfied— I ain't happy no mo' And I wish t
ad died.""I got the Weary Blue And I can't be satisfie
ne Weary Blues And can't be satisfied— I ain't happy
nd I wish that I had died.""I got the Weary Blue And I
e satisfied. Got the Weary Blues And can't be satisfi
in't happy no mo' And I wish that I had died.""I got the
lue And I can't be satisfied. Got the Weary Blues And ca
atisfied— I ain't happy no mo' And I wish that I had di
ot the Weary Blue And I can't be satisfied. Got the Weary
nd can't be satisfied— I ain't happy no mo' And I wish t
ad died.""I got the Weary Blue And I can't be satisfie
ne Weary Blues And can't be satisfied— I ain't happy
nd I wish that I had died.""I got the Weary Blue And I
e satisfied. Got the Weary Blues And can't be satisfi
in't happy no mo' And I wish that I had died.""I got the
lue And I can't be satisfied. Got the Weary Blues And ca

Introduction

It might be said that Langston Hughes's career began in eighth grade. It was then, at Central School in Lincoln, Illinois, that Hughes composed his first poem and gave a public reading of it. It was a sixteen-line tribute to the teachers and students at Central. His first published poem, "The Negro Speaks of Rivers," came years later, however, and it was that poem which caught the attention of Jessie Fauset, literary editor of *Crisis* magazine. She seemed to have an ear for new talent. Fauset quickly became Hughes's most ardent booster. After the success of "The Negro Speaks of Rivers," Fauset published Hughes's work frequently in her magazine.

Although Hughes won great admiration from Fauset and a small circle of Harlem writers and patrons with "The Negro Speaks of Rivers," most scholars put the formal beginning of his career at the 1926 publication of his first book of verse, *The Weary Blues*. This book established Hughes as a blues poet dedicated to bringing poetic respectability to the lives of ordinary working-class African Americans—their joys, their struggles, their soulful laughter, and their blues. Throughout his forty-year career, Hughes wrote countless poems, short stories, plays, librettos, two novels, children's books, a history of the NAACP, and a two-volume autobiography. No other writer of the Harlem Renaissance era endured as long as Hughes, nor was any as prolific.

"THE NEGRO SPEAKS OF RIVERS," THE FIRST POEM OF HUGHES'S THAT WAS EVER PUBLISHED, WAS SET TO MUSIC IN 1960.

During his career, critics of Hughes varied widely in their opinions of the merit of each of his major works. Even though he succeeded in the theater, with more than one of his plays landing on Broadway, it is for his poetry, far more than any of the other genres he worked in, that Hughes is most remembered. Today, most people agree that *The Weary Blues* launched not only Hughes's inimitable career, but also a movement of black creative genius that refused apology for its pride in all things black. A second book, *Fine Clothes to the Jew*, followed close on the heels of *The Weary Blues*. *Not Without Laughter*, Hughes's third book, was also his first novel and earned him the Harmon Award for Literature, a prize of four hundred dollars.

Hughes was one of the first African-American writers to earn a living through his writing. For most of his career, though, he struggled financially. Hughes's reputation was far more significant than his earnings as an artist. For years, he looked for his work to bring him commercial success and make living easy. It never did. Hughes's friends had predicted that his autobiography, *The Big Sea*, would earn him a windfall. Chronically short of cash, Hughes wanted nothing more than for his autobiography to be a big, moneymaking success. But he was to be let down in a major way. *The Big Sea* sold poorly. It was probably the overnight success of a newcomer to New York, a young novelist named Richard Wright, that shattered Hughes's dreams for *The Big Sea*. Wright's first novel was a huge sensation. By the end of 1940 Wright's *Native Son* had sold more than one hundred times as many copies as Hughes's book. In Hughes's own eyes, it set "a new standard for Negro writers" (quoted in Rampersad, 1.383) that *The Big Sea*, for all of its adventure, did not reach in raw power. The failure of *The Big Sea* was the biggest letdown of Hughes's life. Depression set in. It was a demon Hughes would have to battle for years afterward. The deeply felt conflict between his calling as an artist and the struggle to earn a living by it made for Hughes's own blues existence.

Perhaps it is just as well. For almost all of Hughes's career, the poet dedicated himself to catching the spirit of the blues—and its sister art, jazz—in the mood and sentiment of his happy-sad words. His own life was possibly his best inspiration.

THE PUBLICATION OF *THE WEARY BLUES*, HIS FIRST BOOK OF POETRY, PUT HUGHES ON THE MAP AS A MAJOR POET.

Chapter 1

Poetic Works

The Weary Blues

Although his appeal to African Americans, especially the black middle class, surged and receded over time, Langston Hughes was nevertheless black America's poet laureate for more than forty years. His writings over those years, from 1926 to 1967, were massive and as varied in genre as they were extensive in volume. As one critic noted, "His writing spanned all classes and divisions of literature—books, poems, short stories, books edited, works in foreign languages for which there is no English edition, plays, and articles in both journals and in books edited by other scholars" (Taylor, 96). As an exhaustive look at Hughes's writings would far exceed the limits of the objectives set forth, only his major works and genres will be discussed here.

Hughes entered the American literary scene with a splash. His rise to national and international celebrity was hardly a gradual ascent. On the contrary, it was meteoric. In fact, it would not be an overstatement to say, indeed, that Hughes's first book, a collection of original and previously published poems called *The Weary Blues*, took Harlem, the country, and the publishing world by storm.

The Weary Blues: Content and Context

The Weary Blues was published the same year Hughes entered Lincoln University. He was twenty-four years old. The inspiration for the poems in this volume might be said to be related to Hughes's ambitions at another historical black college, Howard University in Washington, D.C. On moving to Washington from New York in 1924, though, Hughes found a different sort of school in the Seventh Street district and it suited him fine. It was the school of the black masses, the life lived by the everyday black folk who came to Washington from the south on only pennies and prayers. Many of the poems included in *The Weary Blues* were inspired by the blues Hughes saw and heard in the nation's capital city. But he was back in Harlem, "in a little cabaret," before he found the precise poetic voice that would become *The Weary Blues*.

Published with the help of Carl Van Vechten by the prestigious Knopf publishing house, *The Weary Blues* distinguished itself by making the lowdownness of blues and jazz music its overarching theme, motif, and meter. The book's title poem, "The Weary Blues," exemplified the general character of the whole collection. It portrayed an old bluesman at his piano, "[d]roning a drowsy syncopated tune, Rocking back and forth to a mellow croon," while he bemoaned his lonely life to the tune of a blues that was the first Hughes had ever heard as a kid in Lawrence, Kansas. Several lines into the poem, we hear the crooning piano man sing the blues Hughes remembers:

> "*I got the Weary Blues*
> *And I can't be satisfied.*
> *Got the Weary Blues*
> *And can't be satisfied—*
> *I ain't happy no mo'*
> *And I wish that I had died.*"
> (*Collected Poems*, 50)

The larger poem follows the structure and meter of classic eight- and twelve-bar blues compositions and is full of the syncopated rhythms of that art form. As Rampersad writes, Hughes relied on "the cadences of urban black speech, derived from the South, with its glissandos, arpeggios, and sudden, unconventional stops" (1.65) in composing one of the most memorable poems of his career, though of course there were several more. With "The Weary Blues," Hughes linked the blues, then music of the black lower class, to the poetic arts of the leisure class, "in order that its brilliance might be recognized by the world" (Rampersad, 1.66).

It was an accident that the second poem in Hughes's volume, "Jazzonia," extended the blues-and-jazz emphasis of "The Weary Blues" with a near-identical musical instinct. Although "Jazzonia" was less rhythmically expressive than "The Weary Blues," its "six long-headed jazzers play[ing]" alerted Hughes's readers that the book's title was meant to encompass more than the title of a single poem opening the collection. Indeed, more than a few of the poems included in *The Weary Blues* evoked the sights and sounds of Harlem's blues clubs and jazz cafés where the "poetry" of the people was sung and played nightly. "To Midnight Nan at Leroy's" ("Sing your blues song,/Pretty baby"), "Harlem Night Club," and "Blues Fantasy" ("Hey! Hey! / That's what the / Blues singers say") cemented Hughes's purpose to highlight the expressive flamboyance of the Harlem social scene in familiar and innovative poetic forms. But *The Weary Blues* was not only a book of blues and jazz verse, nor was it only expressive of the vitality of Harlem. It also included works that might be best thought of as conveying a sense of historical consciousness "deeper" than the high life of Harlem in the 1920s. At least one poem, "The South," spoke intensely of the black American's ambivalent relationship to the South:

The magnolia-scented South.
Beautiful, like a woman,

And I, who am black, would love her
But she spits in my face.
(*Collected Poems*, 27)

Other poems, like "Lament for Dark Peoples" and "Danse Africaine," recalled the black American's African past with equal intensity of feeling. But none of the poems in *The Weary Blues* exemplified the "deeper" sensibility of the poet so closely as "The Negro Speaks of Rivers." First published in the NAACP's *Crisis* magazine, "The Negro Speaks of Rivers" was dedicated to W. E. B. DuBois and expressed Hughes's sense of a deep-seated connection to his African and African-American roots.

Perhaps only the proud poem "I, Too," the last included in *The Weary Blues*, is as well-known today as "The Negro Speaks of Rivers." Although it does not formally compose a blues song, its mood does reflect the tragicomedy of so many blues songs. It poignantly prophecies the end of African-American second-class citizenship:

I, too, sing America.

I am the darker brother.
They send me to eat in the kitchen
When company comes,
But I laugh,
And eat well,
And grow strong.
Tomorrow,
I'll be at the table
When company comes.
Nobody'll dare
Say to me,
"Eat in the kitchen,"
Then.

Besides,
They'll see how beautiful I am
And be ashamed—

I, too, am America. (*Collected Poems*, 46)

Without question, the publication of *The Weary Blues* secured Hughes's significance and catapulted him well past Harlem recognition.

Critical Reaction to *The Weary Blues*

Because it was put out by a major publisher, *The Weary Blues* immediately attracted the attention of the nation's major book reviewers. The *New York Times*, the *New Republic*, the *Herald Tribune*, and the *New Orleans Times-Picayune* all carried favorable reviews of Hughes's first collection. Others had mixed opinions. The *New York Times Literary Supplement* characterized some of the poems in *The Weary Blues* as "superficial" and "sentimental" (quoted in Taylor, 93). Reviews by some black critics, however, were less ambivalent. A number of them—complaining that Hughes's poetic preoccupation with "the strange music of the unlettered Negro" only exposed the underside of black life and did nothing to advance the hope of social progress—were downright damning (Charles Johnson quoted in Taylor, 93). For a large part of the black middle class, the blues was simply too unseemly to be the stuff of poetry.

Still, *The Weary Blues* triumphed. Some in the black literary circles whose company Hughes enjoyed thought very highly of his poems. In *Opportunity*, Jesse Fauset and Alain Locke gave it positive reviews. Hughes's friend Claude McKay spoke of Hughes's achievement in entirely glowing terms: "You have opened up new vistas by touching a subject that thousands of Afro-Americans feel and yet would be afraid to touch" (quoted in Rampersad, 1.129). Apparently, McKay's sentiments were also felt far wider. Translations and compliments came from France, Belgium, Germany, and Central Europe not long after the release of *The Weary Blues*. Since then, Hughes has become one of America's most translated poets. Today, his works are translated in over sixty languages, a trend that began eighty years ago by the transnational notice of *The Weary Blues*.

Fine Clothes to the Jew

Like a good part of *The Weary Blues*, the poems in *Fine Clothes to the Jew* take on the mission of the blues. Hughes seems intent upon finding recognition, validation, and laughter in the lives of urban blacks, while also documenting dispossession, isolation, and despair. A sort of movement from the section "Blues" to "And Blues" through "Railroad Avenue", "Glory! Hallelujah!", "Beale Street Love," and "From the Georgia Roads" carries *Fine Clothes to the Jew* forward.

"Blues"

This section begins with the poem "Hey!," which establishes sundown as the beginning of blues-time, and asks, "wonder what de blues'll bring?" The poems in this section go on to address the specific but generally recognizable hardships of a chorus of people. The poem "Hard Luck" explicitly calls up the problem of selling clothes to the Jewish shop owner to support an alcohol habit and the added trouble of trying to find work. "Misery" and "Suicide" give lyrical voice to a couple of women who have lost the will to live because their men have done them wrong and left them. "Bad Man" speaks back to these in the voice of an abusive alcoholic man who beats his wife "and ma side gal too," with no intentions of changing his ways. A veritable chorus of blues voices, unlucky in love, follows: a woman sets out to a life of wandering because wandering is the only way to escape the "disease" of love; a male voice relates his distress about losing his mind and his money because of a woman he should not have trusted; another malcontent, it seems, dreams of hopping a train home every time the train whistle blows.

"Railroad Avenue"

In the "Railroad Avenue" section of *Fine Clothes to the Jew* Hughes reflects poetically on so many of the unanticipated consequences of northern migration. This section catalogs the vices that are concentrated in the new urban setting

HUGHES CEMENTED HIS BLOSSOMING POETIC REPUTATION WITH THE PUBLICATION OF *FINE CLOTHES TO THE JEW* IN 1926.

and shows a concern for the difficulties of the migrant newcomer trying to navigate the troubled job market in the city. "Brass Spittoons," in fact, relates the thoughts of a man who wants to imagine that his job shining spittoons is somehow worthy work in the sight of God, but is awakened from dreaming by the shrill voices of customers calling out "hey boy" to him. The unholiness of working to serve the wants and needs of white people is extended in "Ruby Brown," the third-person story of a girl who, due to a lack of options and "fuel for the clean flame of joy / that tried to burn within her soul," falls from the ambivalent grace of being a domestic worker to become a prostitute for the exclusive pleasures of white men.

"Prize Fighter" and "Crap Game" return Hughes's readers to the problem of work and the economic insecurity of the city. Similarly, "Elevator Boy" and "Porter" go back into the minds of laborers, the first describing the transience of work and the second extending the social logic of "Brass Spittoons." That is, in "Porter" the man's thoughts are punctuated by his compulsory repetition of the phrase "yes sir," which must be what the spittoon shiner answers to "hey boy."

Perhaps most sadly, even leisure time becomes bankrupt in the "Railroad Avenue" section. The poem "Sport" imagines the emptiness of the life of a person who lives for the nightclub. With a fatalistic tenor, "Saturday Night" exhorts the people in the nightclub to dance and drink and play to no end because, despite everything, death is permanent.

"Glory! Hallelujah!"

Hughes's "Judgment Day" opens the next section. It is obvious why. "Judgment Day" appears to deny the claim made by "Saturday Night," which closes the "Railroad Avenue" section that death is permanent. Instead, it describes the split between the soul and the body in the voice of someone whose soul has arrived to meet God, "clean an' bright." Consistent with Hughes's much-neglected engagement with African-American spirituals and black religious expression, "Prayer Meeting" depicts a "black old woman" heralding the dawn in Ebacaneezer Baptist Church. "Feet O' Jesus" and "Prayer" beg Jesus for mercy and connection and profess a profound not-knowing in the face of God, respectively. By contrast, in three lines "Shout" demands that Jesus listen to his "prophets" and "saints." The latter poems of this section follow the religious theme closely. One of them, "Sinner"—revealing a kinship between religious lament and the blues—asks a god partial to whiteness to have mercy on the sinner who is "po' and black."

"Beale Street Love"

This section returns to the tragic love themes of earlier sections. It opens with abuse and a detailed image of a man punching a woman, who replies, "hit me again." The cycle of love is a cycle of pain. "Cora" attempts to end this cycle by shutting and locking the door to protect her broken heart. "Workin' Man" is a complaint that the woman who is to be the love-refuge from the abusive grind of manual labor is instead a "'hore" who keeps the home looking like a hovel. The poet's domestic preoccupation in the "Beale Street Love" section does not end in "Workin' Man," however. "Baby" assumes the voice of an adult caretaker asking baby Albert to stay out of the street. Albert, too, is subject to the urban carelessness that makes love hazardous.

"From the Georgia Roads"

The theme of the poems in this section is the tortured beauty and tragic realism of the South. "Magnolia Flowers" suggests the increasing difficulty of finding the South beautiful. "Mulatto" juxtaposes the voice of a mulatto who is insisting, "I am your son, white man!" with the voices of southern men who insist, "Niggers ain't my brother." "Song for a Dark Girl" reveals the price of this glamour by describing a black woman lamenting the loss of her lynched lover. Still, for all the tragedy of a region inescapably haunted by the horrors of such racial violence as lynching, the final poem in this section, "Laughers," insists on black joy, and on black people as not tragic, but heroic. They are dancers, singers, and "loud laughers in the hands of Fate."

"And Blues"

This final section of Fine Clothes to the Jew revisits the theme of lost love and recasts its poems in the classic form and mood of the blues. "Lament over Love" is the song of a suicidal mother who hopes that her child never falls in love with a man. "Midwinter Blues" is the lament of a scorned lover whose man has been inconsiderate enough to leave her in the winter when she needs his love the most. The poem "Hard Daddy" echoes "Midwinter Blues" inasmuch as it describes the predicament of a woman whose lover will not comfort her in her time of need. In Hughes's work, not all the men are bad this way, though. "Ma Man," in fact, is a rare poem of praise for a beloved man with "'lectric-shockin' eyes" and great skills as a banjo player. The poem "Hey! Hey!" closes out the collection. It recalls the opening poem of the volume "Hey!" with its imagery of sunset, and evokes instead the sunrise. The blues is a nighttime condition. The sunrise of "Hey! Hey!" offers the respite of day, though surely another sunset is coming.

Critical Reaction to Fine Clothes to the Jew

When the first copies of *Fine Clothes to the Jew* arrived, it was January 1927. Early reviews were good. Charles Johnson praised Hughes for "a final, frank turning to the folk life of the Negro, [for] striving to catch and give back to the world the strange music of the unlettered Negro—his 'Blues'" (quoted in Taylor, 93). Among black critics, though, Johnson's favorable opinion of *Fine Clothes to the Jew* was clearly the exception. Most black critics did not like what they saw as the mean and dirty picture of black people in these poems. Their anger at Hughes was strong: a review in one black newspaper, the Pittsburgh *Courier*, was headlined as "Hughes' Book of Poems Trash." A critic for New York's *Amsterdam News* declared that the book could only have been written by a "sewer dweller." In the black Chicago *Whip*, *Fine Clothes to the Jew* earned Hughes the disparaging title, "the poet lowrate of Harlem" (quoted in Taylor, 93).

The most disparaging critics accused Hughes of selling out his race to white people who enjoyed reading about black people in the gutters. Hearing negative comments from other blacks was obviously painful for Hughes, but as the writer of "The Negro Artist and the Racial Mountain," it didn't truly affect him. In the face of it all, Hughes seemed fearless. His courage was soon rewarded. Before long the tide of opinion about *Fine Clothes to the Jew* shifted, and black and white critics were once again singing Hughes's praises.

Praised or attacked, Hughes was clear about his poetic mission. He was going to write poetry that was direct, clear, and simple enough for uneducated masses, black and white, to read and enjoy. He was going to depict blacks of the lower class no matter who complained. He was going to use his poetry as a platform to protest their conditions on the page and at the microphone. He was going to challenge racial prejudice head on.

HUGHES COMPLETED *NOT WITHOUT LAUGHTER*, HIS FIRST
NOVEL, IN 1930. HE HAD BARELY GRADUATED FROM COLLEGE
AT THE TIME.

Chapter 2

Prose Works

Fiction: *Not Without Laughter*

Langston Hughes completed his first novel, *Not Without Laughter*, in 1930, not long after graduating from Lincoln University. Its simple language and deep feeling pleased almost everyone. It seemed to capture ordinary black life more faithfully than any other novel published in the previous ten years. "Within its limitations as the vicarious autobiography of a boy told in traditional form," writes Arnold Rampersad, "*Not Without Laughter* was perhaps the most appealing and completely realized novel in black fiction to that date." None of Hughes's other attempts at narrative forms would succeed so well. In spite of the wide appeal of *Not Without Laughter*, Hughes's poetry remained his more popular work. Probably the disappointment of his other attempts at narrative writing, including the short story collection *The Ways of White Folks* four years after *Not Without Laughter*, kept Hughes's identity as a poet firmly fixed in his readers' imaginations.

Not Without Laughter tells the story of a typical African-American family from the Midwest. Much of the novel was based on Hughes's childhood in Kansas. The loneliness of the main character, a brown-skinned boy named Sandy, was Hughes's loneliness as a small boy. In the novel, Sandy leaves Kansas for Chicago, just as Hughes had many years earlier. Other characters share similarities with Hughes's own family members. Aunt Hager, a bit like Hughes's grandmother, Mary Langston, was a strong woman with three adult daughters. One of her daughters was Annjee, Sandy's mother, who is a simple, unexciting woman. Annjee's two sisters are more intriguing characters. One is cold and self-centered; the other thinks nothing is so important as singing, dancing, and men. Jimboy is Sandy's father in the novel. Hughes portrays Jimboy as a bluesman and a wanderer, a man with a beautiful singing voice and a love of the road. The world of *Not Without Laughter* is a world of blacks and whites, to be sure, but it is also a world in which skin color among the black characters is a rich spectrum. It is a world in which the beauty of biracial or "yaller" characters (Jimboy Rodgers) is presumed because of their skin's nearness to white. It is a world in which the looks of brown-skinned characters (Sandy Rodgers) are admired because they are not the dark-skinned ones (Annjee Rodgers, Aunt Hager Williams, Willie-Mae Johnson), whose beauty is, in the universe of Hughes's novel, rarely granted.

Plot Summary

Chapter 1

A storm comes in the form of a cyclone that dismantles Aunt Hager's house. She is black and her grandson Sandy, who is brown, wait out the storm in their soon-to-be wrecked house, hoping Sandy's mother, Annjee, is all right walking home. They pray for the safety of Annjee's sisters, Tempy and Harriett. In the aftermath, white neighbors, the Gavitts, are found dead, and the property damage is great.

Chapter 2

Aunt Hager's family lives in the town of Stanton, and Sandy's playmate is a blond and blue-eyed colored boy.

Aunt Hager and Sister Whiteside eat and discuss Annjee's husband, Jimboy, a "yaller" fellow who is, to Aunt Hager, "good-for-nothing." A letter arrives from Jimboy, postmarked Kansas City. The townspeople also talk about Aunt Hager's eldest daughter, Tempy, married to a mail carrier and leaving the Baptists for the higher-class Episcopalian Church.

Chapter 3
Annjee doesn't blame Jimboy for always going away; there is no good work for colored men to be had in Stanton. She feels lucky that she, a dark woman, has a light husband and a brown child. She is proud to have achieved a beautiful family. Public image is important to her.

Chapter 4
Harriett comes home, quitting the good job she has at the country club so she can spend more time partying. She and her mother get into a fight, which ends with Harriett defiantly donning powder, perfume, a blue dress, and red silk stockings like a "black porcelain doll in a Vienna toy shop" (1941, 43).

Chapter 5
Jimboy ignores Annjee while he plays the guitar all night and dances with Harriett in an innocent fashion. Aunt Hager wishes he'd play something holier, more church-appropriate, but Jimboy's songs are about not finding work or being on the chain gang.

Chapter 6
Jimboy is laid off from bricklaying because the white workers won't work with him. Instead, he takes Sandy

fishing. At 5:00 p.m., Sandy remembers he's to help his mother with dishes so she can get ready for a party, and he goes to Mrs. Rice's, where his mother works in the kitchen. There, the white folks are particular and complaining, never thanking Annjee, and Sandy cries.

Chapter 7
Aunt Hager has a new porch built for thirty-five dollars when she makes seventy-five cents a week on laundry, and is the only one of the family who does not hate white folks. Sister Johnson tells how Crowville's houses were burned down, Jimboy speaks of union discrimination, and Harriett of segregation.

Chapter 8
Harriett sneaks out with her boyfriend Mingo to a dance with Sandy in tow. They stay out until dawn with Sandy observing the politics of color: a mustard-colored man slaps a black woman and leaves with a woman the color of maple sugar.

Chapter 9
Jimboy takes Sandy to a carnival. It's a sham, and Sandy sees Harriett dancing for white men, but he'll never tell. He also sees a minstrel show. Harriett runs away with the carnival.

Chapter 10
Sandy goes to the doctor for his festering heel—he's stepped on a rusty nail and is missing Harriett. Jimboy doesn't play the guitar anymore but just loafs. He calls Sandy a liar when the boy spends his Sunday school nickel for candy.

Chapter 11
Sandy enters fifth grade, which is the "white" class, the first level where the teachers (and students) are white. He

is made to sit in the back, the only black boy. When he gets home, Jimboy is gone.

Chapter 12
Annjee gets sick with a chest cold, and Aunt Hager has to take on more washing. Still no word from Jimboy, but Harriett sends a letter ten days before Christmas asking for fare to come home.

Chapter 13
Aunt Hager and Annjee conspire with Brother Logan to get a sled made for Sandy, as the Christmas money was sent to Harriett.

Chapter 14
Sandy is promoted to fifth form A, Annjee returns to Mrs. Rice's, and Harriett comes home. Worried that she will not be able to abide by Aunt Hager's expectations of her and not a little ashamed of her fast life, Harriett opts not to stay with her family despite the excitement of her homecoming. Instead, she moves in with her old friend, Maudel.

Chapter 15
Annjee gets a letter from Jimboy in Detroit and makes up her mind to go to him so he can't keep leaving her. Sandy wishes to be white—though his friend Buster looks white and is considered colored.

Chapter 16
Aunt Hager talks about the white people she's known, storytelling in her new lonely state, and concludes that love is better than hate.

Chapter 17
The family takes in a roomer named Wim Dogberry, a brick mason and coal carrier. Sandy gets a Saturday job in

a barbershop and learns to joke with men and slick down his sandy hair. Overhearing the older men's conversations, Sandy learns that Harriett is a notoriously promiscuous woman.

Chapter 18

An amusement park opens in town (Stanton, Kansas). It announces a Free Children's Day Party for all children with a coupon clipped from the newspaper. Although the paper did not say so, the Children's Day Party was not open to so-called colored children. It was a party for white children only. Sandy and his friend Willie-Mae are denied entrance. A letter for Sandy arrives from his mother, Annjee, who is struggling to survive in Detroit.

Chapter 19

Sandy is offered a job in a hotel as a shoeshine boy and gofer, but Aunt Hager forbids it. In her mind, hotels are disreputable places full of bad men and women. A news item from the evening newspaper suddenly catches their attention. Aunt Hager is aghast: Harriett and Maudel Smothers have been arrested for streetwalking.

Chapter 20

Sandy is asked to bring people liquor, and then, when shining shoes, is subjected to ugly stories and asked to dance for the company. When he refuses, he is verbally abused, and as this abuse escalates, Sandy throws his shoeshine box at the white men and runs off.

Chapter 21

Sandy finds his grandmother taking a break from her washing. She is ill. He calls on Tempy, the eldest aunt, who in turn sends for Annjee and Harriett. Sandy must go to the Bottoms, a red-light district, to find Harriett.

Chapter 22
Aunt Hager's illness is terminal. She is soon dead. Annjee
misses the funeral because she has moved to Detroit without
notice and no one is able to locate her. Harriett promises
her devotion to her now-dead mother, and Tempy arranges
to have Sandy stay with her.

Chapter 23
Sandy moves in with Tempy. For the first time, he has his
own room. Image is important to Tempy and her husband.
Although they are not exactly wealthy, they shop in the
town's better stores. Tempy is intent upon improving
Sandy's image: She calls Sandy James and attempts to
segregate him from his old friends, who aren't attending
high school, as he is, but are out working and playing.

Chapter 24
Sandy gets the mumps. Tempy wants Sandy to look up to
W. E. B. DuBois, the distinguished race leader and
outspoken intellectual, whereas Aunt Hager had wanted
Sandy to model himself on the more conservative Booker
T. Washington, a favorite of white Americans, for a model
of respectable manhood. Tempy finds Sandy a job as a
delivery boy in a card/print shop where there is a lending
library on the side. Sandy begins reading novels from
the library and excels in school, winning second prize in an
essay contest. He also takes a liking to a girl, Pansetta.

Chapter 25
The pool hall was the only place for young colored men (as
African Americans were then called) to go for recreation
in Stanton. The more respectable recreation centers such
as the YMCA were open to white men only. In the pool
hall Sandy hears ribald stories and comes across a news
clipping that Harriett is finding success in musical theater.

Chapter 26
Annjee writes and wants to send for Sandy now that Jimboy is fighting the war in France. Tempy wants Sandy to have nice friends, and Buster is planning to pass for white as his way out and up.

Chapter 27
Warned by Tempy about Pansetta's loose ways, Sandy breaks up with her, then feels bad and decides to visit her at her house. There he finds Pansetta and his friend Jimmy Lane making out. Sandy is stunned. Much to Sandy's dismay, Pansetta, Jimmy informs him, is "easy."

Chapter 28
Annjee finally sends for Sandy after hearing that he is being resistant to Tempy's moral instruction. Sandy is excited to go to Chicago, where Annjee has recently moved. Chicago, however, is a dark and dangerous place. Sandy must navigate his new environment carefully. He is propositioned, in turn, by an older man, an unattractive girl outside the theater, and a prostitute.

Chapter 29
Sandy finds his job as an elevator boy in a Chicago hotel repetitious and interminable, and cannot seem to save up money to afford to return to high school. He promises himself not to be like his father, and not to disappoint Aunt Hager.

Chapter 30
Annjee and Sandy hear Harriett sing at a local Chicago theater. Afterward they grab dinner at a Chinese café. Harriett explains that she's doing well now because, unlike white theater owners, Jewish theater owners are giving black acts a real chance in the business. Harriett insists on supporting Sandy so he can return to school. Annjee

accepts Harriett's help and the novel ends on the bright note of promise. Sandy will return to school, but it is the memory of Stanton, not the false promised land of Chicago, that is his final inspiration.

Major Themes in *Not Without Laughter*

Not Without Laughter was met with considerable praise when it was first published. Many critics were keenly attuned to the novel's coming-of-age concerns: innocence, self-knowledge, and the struggle for independence. The novel, however, is not only about Sandy Rodgers's coming-of-age, it is also about the coming-of-age of all of black America at the beginning of the twentieth century. The heroism of everyday black life and the dignity in black suffering are themes characteristic of Hughes's poetry that are also elegantly expressed in *Not Without Laughter*. Against the backdrop of a rural-to-urban migration motif, these were the blues themes Hughes returned to again and again. The novel's last scene—one in which the fervent music of a small southern church on a Chicago side street reaches Sandy and his mother as they walk into the night toward home—emphasizes Hughes's belief that beauty is often found in the most unexpected places.

Drama: *Mule Bone*

Based on a short story by Zora Neale Hurston called "The Bone of Contention," *Mule Bone* was a collaboration between Hughes and Hurston. It was conceived as a black folk comedy. Shortly after the play's creation in 1930, and unknown to Hughes, Hurston copyrighted the play in her name, excluding Hughes as coauthor. A major conflict followed and a legal battle ensued. Precisely because of those legal issues, *Mule Bone* was not produced during either writer's lifetime. It became a largely forgotten play, though the split between Hughes and Hurston was the stuff of legend in black literary and theater circles. It

BASED ON A SHORT STORY BY ZORA NEALE HURSTON
AND THEN MADE INTO A PLAY WITH THE COLLABORATION
OF HUGHES, *MULE BONE* WAS BURIED IN LEGAL
CONTENTION UNTIL 1991, WHEN IT WAS FINALLY
STAGED IN NEW YORK.

was not until 1991, sixty years after its composition, that *Mule Bone* was finally seen on stage at the Lincoln Center Theater in New York City.

Mule Bone is about two friends, Jim and Dave, who get into a fight over a woman named Daisy. As their fighting escalates, Jim knocks Dave unconscious with a mule bone. Jim is banished from town for two years. Full of wisecracks, folk humor, and southern dialect, *Mule Bone* is high comedy.

Plot Summary

Act 1

As the play begins (and throughout), the town members tease each other about this and that, including aging, sexual prowess, and closeness to God. Mrs. Roberts comes into the store whining and begging for food from the mayor/postmaster/general store owner, Joe Clarke, even though everyone knows that her husband buys more food in the store than anyone in the community. The men in the store brag to each other about the ways that they would discipline Mrs. Roberts if they were married to her.

Next, the town members are found talking about the mule bone that sits on the front porch of the store, and they reminisce about Brazzle's stubborn mule that was "too mean to git fat." Four years ago, at about the time that Joe Clarke opened the store and installed one lamppost, the mule died and was sent off with a big funeral. Therefore, the mule bone is something of a town symbol, reminding everyone (especially Joe) of the way in which the town became a town.

At this point two "town vamps" (Teets and Bootsie), who recently had the attention of their beaux stolen by Miss Daisy Taylor, come into the store/post office to collect and brag about letters from their new, more financially promising boyfriends. Meanwhile, Daisy's brother Senator comes looking for her. The town members suspect that Daisy is off with one or both of her boyfriends, Jim Weston and Dave Carter, who are best friends and presently out performing their two-man show for some "white folks" somewhere. Daisy arrives and is fawned over by all of the men on the porch, who offer to usher her home. She declines and leaves to answer her mother's calls.

Not much later, Jim and Dave come back from their performance and shift from performing for white folks to performing for their own people. The young men begin by complimenting each other on their respective talents at playing the "box," singing, and dancing, but devolve into an argument about who loves Daisy the most. Before long, Daisy comes back to the porch and Jim and Dave fight over who will buy her gum and who will walk her back home, ultimately breaking into song and dance for her attention. They continue to quarrel. Jim trips Dave and also spills a soda that he had purchased for Daisy all over Dave's shirt. They begin to exchange blows and Jim ends the fight by knocking Dave unconscious with the town mule bone.

Act II/ Scene I

Some sisters in the church discuss a notice about a town meeting that Joe, the mayor, has convened to try Jim Weston for assaulting Dave Carter with a "dangerous weapon." The women discuss this as a loyalty issue between the two Christian denominations in the town. The mayor is a Methodist, like Jim, yet he seems to be standing up for Dave, who is a Baptist, and has ordered the trial to be held in the local Baptist church. On their way to the trial, the town members quarrel over matters both religious and personal. The children even break into chants about whose church is the best. The Baptists and Methodists refuse to walk behind each other, so they exit on opposite sites of the stage on their way to the trial.

Act II/ Scene II

The quarreling continues. The mayor fails again and again to bring the town to order. Jim and Dave remark to each other that they have set the whole town fighting. Daisy's mother argues that her child's name is to be kept out of any story about what happened, and indeed Daisy is not at court because she is working. A dozen small arguments start while the people ignore the mayor's attempt to bring order to the room.

Finally, the room becomes quiet enough for the main arguments to be made, and the preachers serve as lawyers against each other. After Dave and Jim recount what happened during their porch fight (awkwardly leaving Daisy's name out of it), the Methodist preacher Simms argues that even though Jim (a Methodist) clearly hit Dave (a Baptist), he cannot be charged with assault. As he has learned by "studying jury" in the "whitefolks court," a mule bone is not a real weapon. He considers the case closed.

However, the Baptist preacher, Elder Childers, counters with an argument based incorrectly on the biblical text of Judges 18:18 (The story is actually in Judges 15:15-16). Childers says that since Samson slew three thousand Philistines with the jawbone of an ass, the mule's hock bone was a dangerous weapon. He concludes that, in fact, based on the Bible, Jim has assaulted Dave with the most dangerous weapon in the world: the mule hock bone.

As judge, Joe is completely convinced by this argument. He banishes Jim from the town for two years and dismisses the court.

Act III
Part of a mob is trying to run Jim out of town. Another part of the mob is trying to keep him in town. Jim ends the struggle by picking up a brick and threatening everyone, declaring that he doesn't want to be a part of such a "ruint" town anyway. As he walks toward nowhere, Daisy appears, evidently to check on Jim. Jim chastises her for the breakup of his friendship with Dave and for conspiring with Dave and the rest of the town to run him out. Daisy denies this charge and convinces Jim that she really wants to be with him. Dave then shows up and Jim is visibly happy until he realizes that Dave has probably come to see Daisy. Dave says that he is not interested in Daisy because she has been two-timing them. The men point out that she

was at Dave's house, rubbing his head after the fight, and in the barn where Jim was held before the trial giving him food. Daisy, upset at them both for yelling at her, is poised to leave. Once again, they both profess divine love to her and convince her to stay. Predictably they begin to quarrel again over who loves her more.

In the end, Daisy chooses Jim and says they should get married immediately. Jim agrees, but he has been exiled from town and Daisy does not want to wander off on some uncharted path with him. She suggests he work as a yardman for the white people, but he refuses. Claiming that she needs a man who is willing to do serious work to support her, Daisy turns to Dave. However, Dave does not want to be a yardman, either. It turns out that neither one of them wants "the job" of supporting Daisy. They each claim to want to keep singing and dancing and wandering forever. Daisy claims to have better offers and rejects both of them. Friends again, Jim and Dave compliment each other on their box-playing and dancing skills and declare their undying loyalty to one another. With the problem of Jim's banishment still before them, Jim and Dave pledge to use whatever amount of mule bone they need in order to insist that Jim be allowed back into town. The men sing and prance offstage together.

Stories: *Simple Speaks His Mind*

Although Hughes regularly represented his hatred of racial prejudice in poems and essays, some of his convictions were expressed in the commonsense speech of a character named Jesse B. Simple (sometimes Jess or Jesse B. Semple), whom Hughes featured regularly in his *Chicago Defender* newspaper column. Much beloved by *Chicago Defender* readers, Simple's popularity led to *Simple Speaks His Mind* in 1950. In the several stories that comprise *Simple Speaks His Mind*, Simple offers comedic folk wisdom on the major

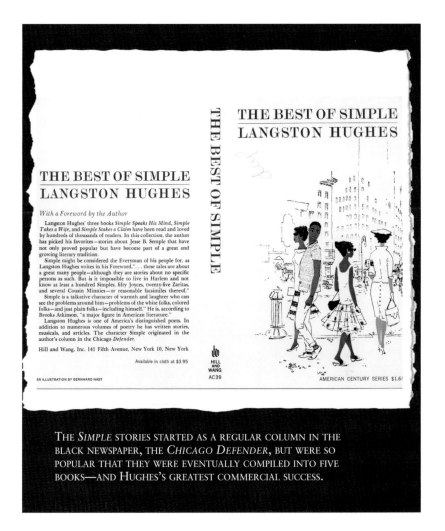

THE *SIMPLE* STORIES STARTED AS A REGULAR COLUMN IN THE BLACK NEWSPAPER, THE *CHICAGO DEFENDER*, BUT WERE SO POPULAR THAT THEY WERE EVENTUALLY COMPILED INTO FIVE BOOKS—AND HUGHES'S GREATEST COMMERCIAL SUCCESS.

political and social issues of his day, including the American hypocrisy surrounding World War II and protection of democracy abroad. *Simple Speaks His Mind* also satirizes the problems of living in Harlem and the "strange" ways of white folks, always with comic precision.

With *Simple Speaks His Mind*, Hughes expected a commercial windfall. It was not an unreasonable expectation.

Early orders for the work numbered 14,000. The reviews of *Simple Speaks His Mind* were almost universally positive. Nearly everyone praised him, writes Rampersad:

> Viewing life most often through the amber haze of a glass beer, Simple managed to convey, in the final analysis, both wisdom and dignity, as well as an unshakable loyalty to his race. Many blacks recognized him immediately as one of them— and recognized also that never before had some like him, with his maddeningly independent point of view . . . gained access to the national forum from which he could pontificate on virtually any subject that crossed his mind. (2.66)

Although sales of *Simple Speaks His Mind* went slowly after the first orders were filled, ultimately 30,000 copies sold. This was not altogether a bad showing, but it hardly amounted to a windfall. Disappointed but undaunted, Hughes refused to give up on Simple. Four more books bearing Simple's name followed: *Simple Takes a Wife* (1953), *Simple Stakes a Claim* (1957), *The Best of Simple* (1961), and *Simple's Uncle Sam* (1965). For more than twenty years, Hughes kept Simple alive and wittily philosophizing. For Hughes, Simple was, just as Arna Bontemps said, "a very happy creation" (quoted in Rampersad, 2.65).

Works

1. Nonfiction

DeCarava, Roy, and Langston Hughes. *The Sweet Flypaper of Life*. New York: Simon & Schuster, 1955. Reprints, New York: Hill and Wang, 1967; Washington, D.C.: Howard University Press, 1984.

Hicks, Granville, Joseph North, Michael Gold, Paul Peters, Isido Schneider, and Alan Calmer, eds. *Proletarian Literature in the United States*. New York: International Publishers, ca. 1935.

Hughes, Langston. *Fight for Freedom: The Story of the NAACP*. New York: Norton, 1962.

———. *A New Song*. Frontispiece by Joe Jones. New York: International Workers Order, ca. 1938.

———. *A Pictorial History of African Americans*. 6th ed. New York: Crown Publishers, ca. 1995.

Hughes, Langston, and Milton Meltzer. *African American History: Four Centuries of Black Life*. New York: Scholastic, 1990.

———. *Black Magic: A Pictorial History of the Negro in American Entertainment*. Englewood Cliffs, NJ: Prentice-Hall, 1967.

Hughes, Langston, Milton Meltzer, and C. Eric Lincoln. *A Pictorial History of Black Americans*. 5th ed. New York: Crown, 1983. Originally published as *A Pictorial History of the Negro in America*.

Nichols, Charles H., ed. *Arna Bontempts—Langston Hughes Letters 1925-1967*. New York: Dodd, Mead, ca. 1980.

2. Fiction

Hughes, Langston. *Laughing to Keep from Crying*. 1st ed. New York: Holt, ca. 1952. Reprint, Mattituck, NY: Aeonian Press, 1976.

————. *Not Without Laughter*. New York:. Knopf, 1930. Reprints, New York: Collier, 1979; New York: Scribner Paperback Fiction, 1995.

————. *The Simple Omnibus*. Mattituck, NY: Aeonian Press, 1978.

————. *Simple Speaks His Mind*. New York: Simon & Schuster, ca. 1950. Reprint, Mattituck, NY: Aeonian Press, 1976.

————. *Simple Stakes a Claim*. New York: Rinehart, ca. 1957.

————. *Simple Takes a Wife*. New York: Simon & Schuster, 1953.

————. *Simple's Uncle Sam*. New York: Hill and Wang, 1967. Reprint, 1977.

————. *Something in Common*. 1st ed. Boston: Houghton Mifflin, 2000.

————. *Tambourines to Glory: A Novel*. New York: Hill and Wang, 1958. Reprint, 1970.
————. *The Ways of White Folks*. 1st ed. New York: Knopf, 1934. Reprints, 1969; New York: Vintage, 1971.

3. Poetry

Braithwaite, Stanley, ed. *Anthology of Magazine Verse for 1928 And Year Book of American Poetry*. New York: Harold Vinal, 1928.

Hughes, Langston. *Ask Your Mama: 12 Moods for Jazz*. 1st ed. New York: Knopf, 1961. Reprint, 1971.

————. *Dear Lovely Death*. Amenia, NY: Troutbeck Press, 1931.

————. *The Dream Keeper and Other Poems*. Illustrated by Helen Sewell. New York: Knopf, 1932. Reprints, 1986, 1994.

————. *Fields of Wonder*. New York: Knopf, 1947.

————. *Fine Clothes to the Jew*. New York: Knopf, 1927.

————. *Freedom's Plow*. New York: Musette, 1943.

————. *Jim Crow's Last Stand*. Atlanta: Negro Publication Society of America, 1943.

————. *Montage of a Dream Deferred*. 1st ed. New York: Henry Holt, 1951.

————. *The Negro Mother, and Other Dramatic Recitations*. Decorations by Prentiss Taylor. New York: Golden Stair Press, 1931. Reprint, Freeport, NY: Books for Libraries Press, 1971.

————. *A New Song*. New York: International Workers Order, 1938.

————. *One-way Ticket*. Illustrated by Jacob Lawrence. 1st ed. New York: Knopf, 1949.

———. *Scottsboro Limited; Four Poems and a Play in Verse.* Illustrated by Prentiss Taylor. New York: Golden Stair Press, 1932.

———. *Selected Poems of Langston Hughes.* New York: Vintage, 1974.

———. *Shakespeare in Harlem.* Drawings by E. McKnight Kauffer. 1st ed. New York: Knopf, 1942.

———. *The Weary Blues.* New York: Knopf, 1926.

4. Juvenilia

Bontemps, Arna, and Langston Hughes. *The Pasteboard Bandit.* Illustrated by Peggy Turley. New York: Oxford University Press, 1997.

———. *Popo and Fifina.* Illustrated by Simms Campbell. New York: Macmillan, 1932. Reprint, New York: Oxford University Press, 1993.

Davis, Ossie. *Langston: A Play.* New York: Delacorte Press, 1982. [Note: Play is about Hughes. He visits a drama group rehearsing one of his plays and uses the actors to recreate scenes from his early life.]

Hughes, Langston. *Black Misery.* Illustrated by Arouni. New York: Eriksson, 1969. Reprint, New York: Oxford University Press, 1994.

———. *The Block: Poems.* Selected by Lowery S. Sims and Daisy Murray Voigt. Collage by Romare Bearden. New York: Viking, 1995.

———. *The Book of Rhythms.* Illustrated by Matthew Wawiorka. Rev. ed. of *The First Book of Rhythms.* New

York: Oxford University Press, 1995.

————. *Carol of the Brown King: Nativity Poems.* Illustrated by Ashley Bryan. New York: Atheneum Books, 1998.

————. *Don't You Turn Back: Poems.* Selected by Lee Bennett Hopkins. Woodcuts by Ann Grifalconi. New York: Knopf, 1969. [Note: Poetry selected by Harlem fourth graders.]

————. *The Dream Keeper and Other Poems.* Illustrations by Helen Sewell. New York: Knopf, 1932. Reprints, 1986, 1994.

————. *The First Book of Africa.* New York: Watts, 1960. Rev. ed., 1964.

————. *The First Book of Jazz.* Music selected by David Martin. Pictures by Cliff Roberts. New York: Watts, ca. 1955; Rev. ed., 1976.

————. *The First Book of Negroes.* Pictures by Ursula Koering. New York: Watts, ca. 1952.

————. *The First Book of Rhythms.* Pictures by Robin King [pseud.]. New York: Watts, 1954.

————. *The First Book of the West Indies.* Pictures by Robert Bruce. New York: Watts, 1956.

————. *Jazz.* Updated and expanded by Sandford Brown. 3rd ed. New York: Watts, 1982. [Note: Earlier edition was *The First Book of Jazz.*]

————. *The Langston Hughes Reader.* 1st ed. New York: Braziller, 1958. Reprint, 1971.

5. Autobiography

Hughes, Langston. *The Big Sea: An Autobiography.* New York: Knopf, 1940. Reprints, New York: Thunder's Mouth Press, 1986; New York: Hill and Wang, 1993.

———. *I Wonder as I Wander: An Autobiographical Journey.* New York: Rinehart, 1956. Reprints, New York: Hill and Wang, 1964; New York: Thunder's Mouth Press, 1986.

6. Collections

Langston Hughes. Presentation par Francois Dodat. Choix de Textes, Bibliographie, Portraits [et] Facsimiles. Paris: Editions P. Seghers, 1964.

Mullen, Edward J., ed. *Langston Hughes in the Hispanic World and Haiti.* Hamden, CT: Archon Books, 1977.

Rampersad, Arnold, ed. *The Collected Works of Langston Hughes.* Columbia: University of Missouri Press, 2001.

7. Edited by Hughes

Hughes, Langston, ed. *An African Treasury: Articles, Essays, Stories, and Poems by Black Africans.* New York: Crown, 1960.

———. *The Best Short Stories by Black Writers; The Classic Anthology from 1899 to 1967.* Boston: Little, Brown, 1969.

———. *The Best Short Stories by Negro Writers; An Anthology from 1899 to the Present.* Boston: Little, Brown, 1967.

———. *The Book of Negro Humor.* New York: Dodd, Mead, 1966.

——— . *Famous American Negroes.* New York: Dodd, Mead, 1954.

——— . *Famous Negro Music Makers.* New York: Dodd, Mead, 1955.

——— . *The New Negro Poets U.S.A.* Bloomington: University of Indiana Press, 1964.

——— . *Poems from Black Africa: Ethiopia, South Rhodesia, Sierra Leone, Madagascar, Ivory Coast, Nigeria, Kenya, Gabon, Senegal, Nyasaland, Mozambique, South Africa, Congo, Ghana, Liberia.* Bloomington: Indiana University Press, 1963.

Hughes, Langston, and Arna Bontemps, eds. *The Book of Negro Folklore.* New York: Dodd, Mead, 1958.

——— . *The Poetry of the Negro, 1746–1970.* 1st ed. Garden City, NY: Doubleday, 1949. Rev. ed., 1970.

8. Translated by Hughes

Guillen, Nicholas. *Cuba Libre, Poems.* Translated by Langston Hughes and Ben Frederic Carruther. Illustrated by Gar Gilbert. Los Angeles: Anderson & Ritchie, 1948.

Lorca, Federico Garcia. *Blood Wedding; and, Yerma.* Translated by Langston Hughes and W. S. Merwin. 1st ed. New York: Theatre Communications Group, 1994.

Reygnault, Christiane, and Langston Hughes. *Anthologie Africaine et Malgache.* Paris: Editions Seghers, 1962.

Rouman, Jacques. *Masters of the Dew.* Translated by Langston Hughes and Mercer Cook. New York: Reynal & Hitchcock, 1947.

9. Operas/Drama

Hughes, Langston. *Black Nativity.* Woodstock, IL: Dramatic, ca. 1992. Original title was *Wasn't That a Mighty Day?*

————. *Freedom's Plow.* New York: Musette, 1943.

————. *Jericho-Jim-Crow-Jericho; A Song-Play.* n.p.: ca. 1963.

————. *Mulatto.* Music by Jan Meyerowitz. n.p.: ca. 1935.

————. *The Negro Mother, and Other Dramatic Recitations.* Decorations by Prentiss Taylor. New York: Golden Stair Press, 1931. Reprint, Freeport, NY: Books for Libraries Press, 1971.

————. *Simply Heavenly.* Music and orchestration by David Martin. New York: Dramatists Play Service, ca. 1959.

————. *Tambourines to Glory.* New York: John Day, ca. 1958.

Hughes, Langston, and Zora Neale Hurston. *Mule Bone: A Comedy of Negro Life.* Edited by George Houston Bass and Henry Louis Gates, Jr. New York: Harper Perennial, 1991.

Revueltas, Silvestre. *Canto de Una Muchacha Negra.* Includes Hughes's "Song for a Dark Girl." New York: Marks Music, 1948.

Smalley, Webster, ed. *Five Plays.* Includes Hughes's "Mulatto," "Soul Gone Home," "Little Ham," "Simply Heavenly," and "Tambourines to Glory." Bloomington: Indiana University Press, 1963.

Stills, William Grant. *Troubled Island: An Opera in Three Acts.* Libretto by Langston Hughes. New York: Leeds Music, ca. 1949.

Three Negro Plays. Includes Hughes's "Mulatto," Baraka's "Slaves," and Hansberry's "Sign in Sidney Brustein's Window." Harmondsworth, UK: Penguin, 1969.

Weill, Kurt. *Street Scenes.* Based on Elmer Rice's play. Lyrics by Langston Hughes. New York: Chappell, 1948.

10. Musical Settings

Barber, Samuel. *Fantasy in Purple.* Words by Langston Hughes. n.p.: 1925.

Bartos, Jan Zdenek. *Koncert Pro Housle a Orchestr.* Original text by Langston Hughes. Praha: Panton, ca. 1974.

Gordon, Ricky Ian. *Genius Child: A Cycle of 10 Songs.* Using poems by Langston Hughes. Milwaukee, WI: Williamson Music, ca. 1995.

———. *Only Heaven: Piano-Vocal.* Milwaukee, WI: Williamson Music, 1997.

Haden, Charlie. *Dream Keeper.* Liberation Music Orchestra. Hollywood: Blue Note, 1991.

Siegmeister, Elie. *Madam to You.* Composers Recordings, CRI SD 416. (P)1979 by Composers Recordings. 1 compact disc.

———. *Ways of Love: Langston Hughes Songs.* Five pieces for piano. Composers Records. (P) 1986 by Composers Recordings. 1 compact disc.

Swanson, Howard. *Seven Songs*. American Recording Society. (P) 1953 by American Recording Society. 1 compact disc.

Weston, Randy. *Bantu*. Read by Langston Hughes. Music by Randy Weston. Roulette RE 130. 2 compact discs.

11. Nonprint Media

America's Town Meeting of the Air. Cataloged from notes compiled by the recording laboratory of the Library of Congress; actual tape contents may vary. Originally broadcast on ABC Radio. 1944. 1 tape reel.

Anthology of Black Poets. Los Angeles, CA: Pacifica Radio Archive, 1983. Audiocassette.

Anthology of Negro Poetry. Read by Arna Wendell Bontemps. Folkways Records FL 9791. Compact disc.

The Beat Generation. Includes "Blues Montage," read by Langston Hughes, with Leonard Feather. Santa Monica, CA: Rhino/Word Beat. (P) 1992 by Rhino/Word Beat. 3 compact discs.

Black Nativity. Read by Marion Williams, Princess Stewart, Alex Bradford, and Langston Hughes. Vee-Jay Records, 196?. Compact disc.

The Dream Keeper and Other Poems. Read by Langston Hughes. Folkways Records FP 104.

The Dream Keeper and Other Poems. Read by Langston Hughes. Folkways Records FC 7104.

Enjoyment of Poetry. Poetry of the Blues. Archive of Recorded Poetry and Literature, Library of Congress, 1963.

The First Album of Jazz for Children, with Documentary Recordings from the Library of Folkways Records. Read by Langston Hughes. Folkways Records FP 712.

The Glory of Negro History. Read by Langston Hughes. Folkways Records FP 752. 1 compact disc.

The Harlem Renaissance and Beyond. VHS. Mt. Kisco, NY: Guidance Associates, ca. 1990.

Hughes, Langston. *The Best of Simple.* Read by the author. Folkways Records FL 9789.

———. *Jericho-Jim Crow.* Read by the author. Folkways Records FL 9671. 2 compact discs.

———. *Langston Hughes Reads and Talks about His Poems.* Read by the author. Spoken Arts SA 1064.

———. *Simple Speaks His Mind.* Read by the author. Folkways Records FP 90. 1 compact disc.

A Langston Hughes Memorial. Los Angeles: Pacifica Radio Archive, 198–. Audiocassette.

Langston Hughes Reading His Poems with Comment, May 1, 1959. Archive of Recorded Poetry and Literature, Library of Congress, 1959. 1 tape reel.

Langston Hughes Videorecording: The Dream Keeper. VHS. South Carolina Educational Television Network, a New York Center for Visual History Production, 1988.

Looking for Langston. VHS. Sankofa Fil and Video. New York: Third World Newsreel, 198–.

Poems from Black Africa. Read by Langston Hughes. Caedmon TC 1315. Audiocassette.

The Poetry of Langston Hughes. Caedmon TC 1272. Audiocassette.

Poetry and Reflections. Read by Langston Hughes. New York: Caedmon, 1980. Audiocassette.

The Spoken Arts Treasury of 100 Modern American Poets Reading Their Poems. Spoken Arts 1040-1057. 18 slipcases.

The Subject Is Jazz. Jazz and Other Arts. First broadcast 1958 by NBC in cooperation with the Educational Television and Radio Center. Produced by Brice Howard. Hosted by Gilbert Seldes with guest Langston Hughes. 3 16 mm tapes.

Tambourines to Glory. Gospel songs by Langston Hughes and Jobe Huntley. Folkways Records FG 3538. 1958.

Filmography

Langston Hughes: His Life and Times. DVD. Films for the Humanities & Sciences, 2003.

Langston Hughes: The Poet In Our Hearts. VHS. Chip Taylor Productions, 1995.

Langston Hughes: Salvation. VHS. Films for the Humanities & Sciences, 2003.

Looking for Langston. VHS. Dir. Isaac Julien. British Film Institute (BFI), Sankofa Film & Video, 1989.

Voices & Visions: Langston Hughes, the Dream Keeper. VHS. Dir. Saint Clair Bourne. New York Center for Visual History, 1988.

Chronology

1902
James Langston Hughes is born to James Nathaniel Hughes and Carrie Langston on February 1 in Joplin, Missouri.

1916
Named "class poet" upon graduating from junior high in Lincoln, Illinois.

1920
Edits yearbook and is once again named "class poet." Graduates from Central High School in Cleveland, Ohio.

1921
"The Negro Speaks of Rivers," his first nationally published work, appears in W. E. B. DuBois' *Crisis*.

After convincing his reluctant father, returns from a summer in Mexico and matriculates at Columbia University in New York.

1922
Becomes increasingly infatuated with Harlem and disgruntled with privileged university life, withdraws from Columbia University.

1923
Becomes a merchant seaman and sails to Africa; is confronted with questions of blackness and racial belonging there.

1925
Publishes some works in Alain Locke's *The New Negro;* the book contributes to Hughes's growing national fame.

Awarded first prize for poetry in the National Urban League's *Opportunity* magazine.

1926
The Weary Blues is published and named after one of his prize-winning poems; the work solidifies his innovatively rhythmic, poetic style.

1927
Publishes *Fine Clothes to the Jew*, a book of poetry panned by white and black critics for its depictions of lower-class blacks.

1929
Earns bachelor's degree from Lincoln University, a historically black college for men, in Pennsylvania; while there, writes an eye-opening piece on the state of race relations at the university.

1930
Under the financial support and encouragement of Godmother Mason, writes his first novel, *Not Without Laughter.*

1931
Takes a year to read; travels through the South lecturing and bringing poetry to the "black masses."

1932
Visits the Soviet Union for an unsuccessful collaborative film project, *Black and White;* writes short fiction and develops a deep interest in communism.

1935
Receives Guggenheim fellowship, allowing him to found Harlem-based theater groups.

1935
Mulatto, one of the longest-running, black-authored plays on Broadway, debuts.

1936
Collaborates with the Gilpin Players, works on producing drama.

1937
Covers the Spanish Civil War as a journalist in Spain.

1940
After working sporadically for years, finally publishes an autobiography, *The Big Sea*.

1942
Moves to Harlem permanently.

1943
Writes for the *Chicago Defender*, creates character Jesse B. Simple (or Semple).

1951
Publishes *Montage of a Dream Deferred*.

1953
Investigated by McCarthy's subcommittee.

1956
Writes play *Tambourines to Glory*.

Publishes *I Wonder as I Wander*, his second auto-biography.

1957
Simply Heavenly appears on Broadway.

1958
In a unique collaborative effort, records poetry over jazz accompaniment provided by bassist Charles Mingus.

1959
Publishes *Selected Poems of Langston Hughes.*

1961
Inducted into National Institute of Arts and Letters.

1963
Supports NAACP in speeches deploring violence.

1966
Represents America at First World Festival of Negro Arts in Dakar, Senegal.

Dies in New York City on May 22 at the age of sixty-five.

Notes

Part I

Chapter 1

p. 13, par. 1, Although the first mass-produced automobiles were not available until 1908, in 1900 there were 8,000 automobiles, mostly handcrafted, registered in the United States. When Ford Motor Company introduced the mass-produced Model T six years after Hughes's birth, it had a price tag of $950. By 1910 Joplin included many self-made men for whom an automobile was not out of reach. "Growth of Range Line, Ford Parallel," the *Joplin Globe*. (July 8, 2003). See also, *Joplin, Missouri: The City That "Jack" Built: Some of Its Business and Its Beauties: 1902.* http://www.joplinpubliclibrary.org/postcards/j02p001th.jpg

p. 15, par. 2, Hughes's second-grade teacher, Mary J. Dillard, called him a "dreamy little boy."

p. 31, par. 2, In Hughes's autobiography this vessel is unnamed. "McKeesport," however, is the fictional name given to the Pennsylvania town "near Pittsburgh" where his mother, stepfather, and stepbrother, Gwyn, were living in 1923.

p. 38, par. 2, "Lincoln is wonderful," Hughes wrote to his fellow poet, Countee Cullen, upon arriving at the little university southwest of Philadelphia (quoted in Rampersad, 1.125).

p. 41, par. 3, Some have wondered at Hughes's title, *Fine Clothes to the Jew*. The title is extracted from his poem "Hard Luck." In the poem, the speaker, down on his luck, resigns to selling his finest clothes to a Jewish used-clothing dealer in order to get some cash. *See* Rampersad, 1.136.

p. 44, par. 2, Hughes was all the more astonished by Godmother Mason's accusations because he was, among her four protégés (including Locke, Hurston, and the black music and composer, Hall Johnson), the only one who had ever been completely honest in his dealings with her.

p. 49, par. 3, In Cleveland, Hughes had other troubles, too. Along with two friends, Hughes would spend a cold January night in a Cleveland jail. The three of them had been falsely accused of doing damage to a taxi driver's cab. When the police arrived on the scene, they urged the three to confess or go to jail. When Hughes and his friends refused to confess to a crime they did not commit, they were rounded up and taken downtown. In the morning they were released without charges, perhaps because of Hughes's fame.

p. 61, par. 1, Four months earlier, the phrase "liberty and justice for all" had been enshrined in legislation officially sanctioning the pledge to the flag. It was cruelly ironic that, as Hughes recognized, "liberty and justice" were not shared by all.

Part II

Chapter 1

p. 86, par. 1, Some years earlier, before he knew anything about Lincoln, Hughes had decided that he should finish college at a black college. His friend Alain Locke was a professor at Howard and would help him get admitted.

p. 86, par. 2, *The Weary Blues* was originally published by the Knopf publishing company. Alfred and Blanche Knopf were close friends of Carl Van Vechten.

Further *Information*

Further Reading

Berry, S. L. *Langston Hughes*. Mankato, MN: Creative Education, 1994.

Cooper, Floyd. *Coming Home: From the Life of Langston Hughes*. New York: Philomel Books, ca. 1994.

Dunham, Montrew. *Langston Hughes: Young Black Poet*. Illustrated by Robert Doremus. New York: Aladdin Paperbacks, 1995.

Hill, Christine M. *Langston Hughes: Poet of the Harlem Renaissance*. Springfield, NJ: Enslow, ca. 1997.

McKissack, Pat, and Fredrick McKissack. *Langston Hughes: Great American Poet*. Hillside, NJ: Enslow, 1992.

Meltzer, Milton. *Langston Hughes: A Biography*. New York: Crowell, 1968.

———. *Langston Hughes*. Illustrated by Stephen Alcorn. Brookfield, CT: Millbrook Press, ca. 1997.

Myers, Elisabeth P. *Langston Hughes: Poet of His People*. Illustrated by Russell Hoover. New York: Dell, 1981.

Osofsky, Audrey. *Free to Dream: The Making of a Poet*. 1st ed. New York: Lothrop, Lee & Shepard, ca. 1996.

Walker, Alice. *Langston Hughes, American Poet*. Illustrated by Don Miller. New York: Crowell, 1974. Reprint, New York: HarperCollins, 1998.

Web Sites
The Academy of American Poets
http://www.poets.org/poet.php/prmPID/83

America's Story: Meet Amazing Americans
http://www.americaslibrary.gov/cgi-bin/page.cgi/aa/hughes

Black History
http://www.galegroup.com/free_resources/bhm/bio/hughes_l.htm

Cora Unashamed
http://www.pbs.org/wgbh/masterpiece/americancollection/cora/hughes_timeline.html

James Langston Hughes
http://www.redhotjazz.com/hughes.html

Langston Hughes Biography
http://www.kansasheritage.org/crossingboundaries/page6e1.html

Langston Hughes (1902–1967) Teacher Resource File
http://falcon.jmu.edu/~ramseyil/hughes.htm

Modern American Poetry: Langston Hughes in the 1930s
http://www.english.uiuc.edu/maps/poets/g_l/hughes/1930s.htm

Bibliography

Works Consulted

Bass, George Houston, and Henry Louis Gates, Jr., eds. *Mule Bone: A Comedy of Negro Life: Edited with Introductions by George Houston Bass and Henry Louis Gates, Jr.* New York: Harper Perennial, 1991.

Bernard, Emily, ed. *Remember Me to Harlem: The Letters of Langston Hughes and Carl Van Vechten, 1924–1964.* New York: Knopf, 2001.

Bontemps, Arna, ed. *The Harlem Renaissance Remembered.* New York: Dodd, Mead, 1972.

DuBois, W. E. B. "Returning Soldiers." *The Portable Harlem Renaissance Reader.* Edited by David Levering Lewis. New York: Penguin, 1994.

Gates, Henry Louis, and Nellie McKay. *The Norton Anthology of African American Literature.* 2nd ed. New York: W. W. Norton, 2004.

Huggins, Nathan Irvin. *Harlem Renaissance.* New York: Oxford University Press, 1971.

————, ed. *Voices from the Harlem Renaissance.* New York: Oxford University Press, 1976.

Hughes, Langston. *The Big Sea: An Autobiography.* New York: Knopf, 1940. Reprints, New York: Thunder's Mouth Press, 1986; New York: Hill and Wang, 1993.

_____. *The Collected Poems of Langston Hughes*. Edited by Arnold Rampersad and David Roessel. New York: Vintage, 1994.

_____. *I Wonder as I Wander: An Autobiographical Journey*. New York: Rinehart, 1956. Reprints, Hill and Wang, 1964; New York: Thunder's Mouth Press, 1986.

_____. "The Negro Artist and the Racial Mountain." The *Nation 23* (June 23, 1926). In *The Portable Harlem Renaissance Reader*. Edited by David Leverling Lewis. New York: Penguin, 1994.

_____. *Not Without Laughter*. New York: Knopf, 1941. Reprints, New York: Collier, 1979; New York: Scribner Paperback Fiction, 1995.

Johnson, Charles S. "The Negro Renaissance and Its Significance." In *The Portable Harlem Renaissance Reader*. Edited by David Levering Lewis. New York: Penguin, 1994.

Johnson, James Weldon. *Black Manhattan*. In *The Portable Harlem Renaissance Reader*. Edited by David Levering Lewis. New York: Penguin, 1994.

Kent, George E. "Patterns of the Harlem Renaissance." *The Harlem Renaissance Remembered*. Edited by Arna Bontemps. New York: Dodd, Mead, 1972.

Leach, Laurie F. *Langston Hughes: A Biography*. Westport, CT: Greenwood Press, 2004.

Lewis, David Levering. *When Harlem Was in Vogue*. New York, Oxford University Press, 1979.

Locke, Alain. *The New Negro: Voices from the Harlem Renaissance*. New York: Macmillan, 1992.

McKay, Claude. "If We Must Die." In *The Norton Anthology of African American Literature*. 2nd ed. Edited by Henry Louis Gates Jr., and Nellie McKay. New York: W. W. Norton, 2004.

Rampersad, Arnold. *The Life of Langston Hughes*. 2nd ed. 2 vols. New York: Oxford University Press, 2002.

Taylor, Patricia E. "Langston Hughes and the Harlem Renaissance, 1921–1931: Major Events and Publications." In *The Harlem Renaissance Remembered*. Edited by Arna Bontemps. New York: Dodd, Mead, 1972.

Index

Page numbers in **boldface** are illustrations, tables, and charts. Proper names of fictional characters are shown by (C).

About the Author

Maurice Wallace is associate professor of English and African Studies at Duke University in Durham, North Carolina. He is the author of *Constructing the Black Masculine: Identity and Ideality in African American Men's Literature and Culture, 1775–1995,* and several articles on African-American literature and culture. *Langston Hughes: The Harlem Renaissance* is Wallace's first book for Marshall Cavendish Benchmark. Hughes has been a favorite poet of Wallace's since childhood. Today, Wallace lives in Durham with his wife, Pam, and two extraordinary daughters, Sage and Amaya.